I Believe

A Concise Guide to the Essentials of the Christian Faith

THOM S. RAINER

TYNDALE
MOMENTUM®

A Tyndale nonfiction imprint

Visit Tyndale online at tyndale.com.

Visit Tyndale Momentum online at tyndalemomentum.com.

Tyndale, Tyndale's quill logo, *Tyndale Momentum*, and the Tyndale Momentum logo are registered trademarks of Tyndale House Ministries. Tyndale Momentum is a nonfiction imprint of Tyndale House Publishers, Carol Stream, Illinois.

I Believe: A Concise Guide to the Essentials of the Christian Faith

For information about special discounts for bulk purchases, please contact Tyndale House Publishers at csresponse@tyndale.com, or call 1-855-277-9400.

Library of Congress Cataloging-in-Publication Data

A catalog record for this book is available from the Library of Congress.

ISBN 978-1-4964-4901-6

Printed in China

29	28	27	26	25	24	23
7	6	5	4	3	2	1

CONTENTS

INTRODUCTION

I did not know where to begin.

I had just become a Christian, and I wanted to know more. I understood the basics of what it meant to be a Christian because my high school football coach had shared the gospel with me.

I knew I was a sinner. I knew that Jesus died on the cross to pay the price for my sins. I knew I could not be a heaven-bound follower of Christ through my own works. I fully understood that my salvation was a gift; I had done nothing to earn it.

I had repented of my sins. I had placed my faith in Christ. I now trusted him to be my Lord and Savior.

But I didn't know what was next.

In my defense, I had never heard about Christian discipleship. For certain, I had never heard the word *sanctification*, which refers to the process of growing as a Christian and becoming more like Jesus.

I would later come to understand that brand-new Christians are often called "baby Christians" because they have just been born into the Christian faith. The apostle Paul writes about these new believers in 1 Corinthians 3:1-2: "Dear brothers and sisters, when I was with you I couldn't talk to you as I would to spiritual people. I had to talk as though you belonged to this world or as though you were infants in Christ. I had to feed you with milk, not with solid food, because you weren't ready for anything stronger."

Paul nailed it. That is exactly how I felt. I was an infant Christian, a new Christian. I needed to be spiritually fed. I was hungry, spiritually hungry. But I didn't know where to turn.

Then I remembered that I had a Bible, which had been given to me at birth. In those days, it wasn't uncommon for family or friends to give a Bible for such occasions. But I'm not sure I had ever opened that Bible. The dedication page still looked crisp and new, with a handwritten inscription from some close friends of the family. But now, as a teenager and for the first time I could recall, I started reading the Bible on my own.

I would be disingenuous to say the process was easy. No one told me, for example, to read the Gospel of John first because of its up-close-and-personal portrayal of Jesus by one of his closest friends. No one guided me to help me understand the more difficult passages in the Bible. To make the challenge greater, the translation I had was the King James Version. I would often read a single verse several times just to get an idea of what it meant.

I think I finally read through the entire Bible, from Genesis to Revelation, but I can't say with certainty that I actually finished it. I don't remember any moment of celebration or sense of accomplishment for reaching Revelation 22:21, the final verse of Scripture.

But even though the reading was often laborious and frustrating, I can say with assurance that the Holy Spirit opened my heart, mind, and eyes on many occasions.

In my early twenties, I discovered a book titled *What the Bible Is All About*, by Henrietta Mears, which provided a clear and concise overview of the totality of Scripture, along with insightful summaries of each of the Bible's sixty-six books. I devoured it with eagerness and excitement.

A major catalyst for growth was connecting to a local church, which didn't happen until after I was married. When I first became a Christian, no one encouraged me to join a church. My small hometown had several, so it wasn't as if there were no opportunities to find one. I just never did. But shortly after Nellie Jo and I got married, she began nudging me to find a church for us to attend.

What I loved about my wife's approach was that it was one of encouragement. She didn't nag. She didn't try to make me feel guilty. She simply encouraged me. She even asked me to take the lead in choosing the church we would join.

It would not be an exaggeration to say that the local church was *essential* to my spiritual growth. I treasured hearing biblical preaching every week. I couldn't wait to study the text we would discuss in my weekly Bible study at church. The natural accountability of the local church was indispensable to my spiritual growth as I learned even deeper truths from God's Word. To continue with the apostle Paul's metaphor, I finally moved from spiritual milk to solid food.

Why have I shared with you a portion of my spiritual autobiography? Because I have been incredibly blessed to have godly people and resources in my life, and I have a keen desire to serve others in a similar fashion. I also love the local church. Each church is imperfect, with imperfect members like me. But the church is God's primary instrument to reach the world and disciple believers.

I envision this book being used primarily in the context of a local church. Perhaps some small groups will make a study of its chapters. Or maybe it will be used in membership classes to make sure that newcomers understand the foundational doctrinal truths of the Christian faith.

But if you desire to know or review the key elements of Christian belief, you may decide just to read the book on your own. That's what I would have done if a similar resource had been available when I became a follower of Jesus.

The truths of the Christian faith are powerfully clear and wonderfully deep. On the one hand, it doesn't take an advanced degree to understand the basics of Christianity, and I pray that this book will speak with clarity to anyone who has a desire to learn. On the other hand, the Christian faith is both rich and deep. I began devouring the truths of Christianity as a young man in my twenties. Now in my sixties, I am still a student of the Bible, and I am amazed at how much I learn every day when I open God's Word with a prayerful and receptive heart. I know I will continue to learn and grow until I see my Savior face-to-face.

Hebrews 4:12 sums it up beautifully: "The word of God is alive and powerful. It is sharper than the sharpest two-edged sword, cutting between soul and spirit, between joint and marrow. It exposes our innermost thoughts and desires." I invite you to open your Bible as you read this brief summary of the beliefs of our faith. I invite you to pray before reading so that you can hear God clearly. I invite you to not only learn cognitively, but ask God how he can use these truths to help you walk more closely with him.

This book is simply called *I Believe*. We will look at some of the most important truths you will ever know because they are God's truths. As we know them better, we understand the nature of God more fully. As we understand the nature of God more fully, we seek to serve him more readily. And as we serve him more readily, he uses us as his servants to be ministers of grace and gospel bearers to others.

Thank you for joining me on this adventure. It is the adventure of a lifetime, and it leads to our transition from this life to eternity.

1

I BELIEVE IN THE BIBLE

A friend of mine inspired me recently. This friend has three grandsons. As of this writing, the boys are ten, seven, and three. Like many of us grandparents, my friend wants to leave a legacy for his grandsons. He had an idea and went to work on it.

First he purchased three note-taking or journaling Bibles. He began reading one of the three Bibles with the intention of reading it through in a year. Not only did he complete the one-year reading goal, but he also took notes in the Bible as he read it each day. At the completion of one year, my friend had an entire Bible with his own handwritten commentary on each page.

Of course, he had purchased three journaling Bibles, so

he repeated the process over the next two years. He plans to leave each grandson one of the Bibles as part of his legacy.

Can you imagine his grandsons reading through their Bibles with their granddad's notes and commentary? Can you imagine how those Bibles will shape those boys into manhood?

Though some of the notes are no doubt similar, they will have differences as well. Perhaps the three brothers will compare their notes on the same passages in the future. In any case, all three boys will have a remarkable gift from someone who loves them dearly.

Here is the key takeaway: When this granddad decided he wanted to leave his grandsons a powerful and meaningful legacy, he chose the Bible. Nothing is as powerful and priceless as the Word of God.

THE BIBLE IS THE WORD OF GOD

Think about those words: The Bible is the Word of God. Every time we open and read the Bible or listen to an audio version, we are hearing from God. His words speak directly to us.

There are numerous passages in the Old Testament that are explicitly from God. For example, read Exodus 4:22-23: "This is what the LORD says: Israel is my firstborn son. I commanded you, 'Let my son go, so he can worship me.'" Or look at Jeremiah 1:9: "The Lord reached out and touched my mouth and said, 'Look, I have put my words in your mouth!'" In some of the translations, these passages begin with the familiar, "Thus says the Lord."

While these examples are direct quotes from God, Paul makes it clear that the totality of Scripture—Old Testament and New Testament—is the inspired Word of God. In his letter to Timothy, Paul writes, "You have been taught the holy Scriptures from childhood, and they have given you the wisdom to receive the salvation that comes by trusting in Christ Jesus. All Scripture is inspired by God and is useful to teach us what is true and to make us realize what is wrong in our lives. It corrects when we are wrong and teaches us to do what is right" (2 Timothy 3:15-16).

All Scripture is inspired by God. Not just some of it. Not just the passages we might perceive as important. Not just the Old Testament passages that say God is speaking. Not just the New Testament passages. Not just the words of Jesus that are sometimes printed in red in our Bibles. *All* Scripture is inspired by God. *All* Scripture is the Word of God.

We can thus read the entirety of the Bible with the full confidence that God is speaking to us. In fact, the words of Scripture are truth itself. When Jesus was praying to God the Father on behalf of believers, he said, "Make them holy by your truth; teach them your word, which is truth" (John 17:17).

The implications of the Bible as the Word of God are staggering. It means we can be confident that we are reading truth and not error. Though the Bible doesn't give us an exhaustive treatment of every subject, and there are scientific details beyond the scope of what the Bible says, we can be certain that the details of what the Bible tells us are true. The Bible doesn't affirm anything that isn't true.

The Bible was written by ordinary men, writing in their ordinary styles. They wrote for a specific context and time. They wrote with their own personalities reflected in their words. But God made certain that they wrote nothing but truth. Indeed, through the process of inspiration, God made certain the Bible is all truth.

THE BIBLE IS INSPIRED

As I was writing this chapter, I paused to listen to an audio text message from my daughter-in-law. She wanted my wife and me to hear one of our young grandsons playing the piano. After we listened to the short audio text, my wife said, "That is such inspirational music."

In another setting, a father of the bride offering a toast to his daughter and new son-in-law says he feels inspired to speak the words he is about to share.

Indeed, we use the words *inspire* and *inspirational* freely—such as when we are trying to motivate someone.

For example, my high school football coach *inspired* me to become a better player. Or we might use those words when we have moments of creativity, like painting a landscape, composing a song, or writing a book. We were *inspired* for those moments of creativity.

Though the various authors of the books of the Bible were undoubtedly motivated to write their books, and they likely had moments of creativity, the inspiration of Scripture goes beyond motivation. As we saw earlier, Paul wrote to Timothy that "all Scripture is inspired by God" (2 Timothy 3:16).

Note that Paul says the *Scripture* is inspired rather than that the *writers* were inspired. In fact, the word *inspired* translated from Greek is a combination of two words: God (*theos*) breathed (*pneustos*). Thus, the inspiration of the Bible is literally the breath of God. Scripture comes from God himself.

Because the words of Scripture came from the breath of God, we can affirm with confidence that they are unequivocally the Word of God. What does that mean for us practically?

First, it means we can read with full confidence that every word is true. We may not always understand every chapter or verse, but that doesn't make them any less true. When we read Scripture, we are hearing from God.

Second, it means that the Bible is authoritative. Because God is the ultimate author, the words we read are coming directly from him. He is the Creator of all and King of all. We do not read the Bible as merely an exercise in theological training. We read the Bible to submit to God, who will change our lives according to his will.

The writer of Hebrews penned these powerful words about Scripture: "The word of God is alive and powerful. It is sharper than the sharpest two-edged sword, cutting between soul and spirit, between joint and marrow. It exposes our innermost thoughts and desires" (Hebrews 4:12).

The Word of God came from the breath of God. It is thus *alive* and *powerful*. This verse also demonstrates how Scripture can affect us and change us. The writer uses the metaphor of a sword that is so sharp it can divide joint from marrow. In other words, it cuts us open spiritually and exposes us completely. We can disobey God's Word, but we cannot ignore it.

Simply stated, the very act of reading the Bible is an act of spiritual surgery. That surgery is meant to expose our deepest thoughts and desires, and it does so that we might be changed toward greater obedience.

Brad Waggoner, author of *The Shape of Faith to Come*, led a massive study on the factors that move us to be more like Christ or to become more devoted followers of the Savior. At the risk of oversimplifying his findings, I was struck by one major discovery: Those who read their Bibles daily are most likely to become committed followers of Christ.

The study found that daily Bible readers will pray more consistently. They will share the gospel more readily. They will be more active in their churches and demonstrate greater commitment to their churches. Do you get the picture? We don't merely learn biblical truths when we read the Bible; we are changed to be more like Christ.

The Bible was inspired by the Holy Spirit. Today, the Holy Spirit convicts us to walk paths of righteousness when we read the Bible faithfully.

THE BIBLE IS NECESSARY

The Bible provides all a person needs to become a Christian and grow as a Christian. But without the Bible, he or she would not know these truths. When we say the Bible is necessary for someone to become a Christian and become a more mature Christian, we mean it is essential to read the Bible, or have someone read the Bible to us and explain it.

The apostle Paul points to this reality when he says of Jesus, "How can they call on him to save them unless they believe in him? And how can they believe in him if they have never heard about him? And how can they hear about him unless someone tells them? And how will anyone go and tell them without being sent? That is why the Scriptures say, 'How beautiful are the feet of messengers who bring good news!'" (Romans 10:14-15). He concludes, "So faith comes from hearing, that is, hearing the Good News about Christ" (Romans 10:17).

Someone has to read Scripture or proclaim Scripture for people to be saved. The story of the Ethiopian eunuch in the book of Acts is telling. The eunuch was reading from the book of Isaiah when Philip approached him and asked him if he understood what he was reading. "The man replied, 'How can I, unless someone instructs me?' And he urged Philip to come up into the carriage and sit with him" (Acts 8:31).

Paul again reminds us that Scripture is necessary for someone to both become a Christian and grow as a Christian: "You must remain faithful to the things you have been taught. You know they are true, for you know you can trust those who taught you. You have been taught the holy Scriptures from childhood, and they have given you the wisdom to receive the salvation that comes by trusting in Christ Jesus" (2 Timothy 3:14-15).

The Bible is also necessary for you to know God's will. God does not give us a precise road map for his will; he desires for us to walk by faith at all times. Still, Scripture reveals much to us about God's plan for our lives and the paths we should take.

John writes, "Everyone who believes that Jesus is the Christ has become a child of God. And everyone who loves the Father loves his children, too. We know we love God's children if we love God and obey his commandments. Loving

God means keeping his commandments, and his commandments are not burdensome" (1 John 5:1-3).

So we learn what God wants for us by keeping his commandments. His commandments, of course, are found in Scripture.

The Bible is necessary. It is necessary for salvation. It is necessary for growth as a Christian. And it is necessary in order to know God's will for our lives.

POSTSCRIPT: A BRIEF WORD ON HOW WE GOT THE BIBLE

We use the word *canon* to describe the inspired books of the Bible. In Greek, the word is *kanon*, which signifies a standard of measure. In other words, the early church councils sought to determine whether certain writings "measured up" to be included in the Bible. It is a misunderstanding to say that these groups or councils caused certain books to be inspired. In those cases where a council met, they recognized which books had already been embraced by the faith community (that is, by Jews for the Old Testament and Christians for the New Testament). Indeed, most of the sixty-six books of the Bible were quickly accepted as the Word of God.

Paul Enns, in *The Moody Handbook of Theology*, does a good job of delineating the tests that were used to determine whether a writing was truly from God and thus worthy of being included as Scripture. The specific tests he notes for the Old Testament are as follows:

- Did the book itself indicate it had God as its author?
- Did the book indicate that God was speaking through a mediator such as a prophet?
- Was the human author clearly a spokesman for God?
- Was the author a prophet or a person with a prophetic gift?
- Was the book historically accurate?
- Ultimately, how was the book received by Jews? That faith community made certain these books, now the thirty-nine Old Testament books, "measured up" to be Scripture.[1]

Enns cites some similar tests for the New Testament books to be included in our Bible:

- Was the author of the book an apostle or did he write under apostolic or prophetic authority? Paul, for example, clearly stated that he was writing with prophetic authority and that his words came from the Lord: "If you claim to be a prophet or think you are spiritual, you should recognize that what I am saying is a command from the Lord himself" (1 Corinthians 14:37).

- Did the churches of the early centuries recognize the authoritative nature of the books? Some were embraced quickly. Some were slower to be recognized. Today, the church clearly recognizes the inclusion and authority of the twenty-seven books of the New Testament.
- Were the books consistent with the teachings and doctrine of the early church? Several books were deemed inconsistent with the witness and teachings of Christ and his closest followers.
- Did the books reflect the quality of inspiration? In other words, they must not waver from the high moral and spiritual values that would demonstrate the work and fruit of the Holy Spirit.
- Was the book used in Christian worship in the early church? Most Christians in the incipient stages of the church could not read. None of the early Christians had copies of Bibles they could read. The early Christians, therefore, depended upon the reading of Scripture in worship services. It is in this context where many of the books of the New Testament were affirmed and confirmed to be the Word of God.[2]

The Bible is the inspired Word of God. It is necessary for the salvation of many and the spiritual growth of all believers. We thus acclaim without hesitation, "I believe in the Bible."

I BELIEVE IN GOD THE FATHER

There is one God. Yet this one God has eternally existed as three persons: God the Father, God the Son (Jesus), and God the Holy Spirit. We call this reality the doctrine of the Trinity, and we will explore it more deeply in chapter 5. For now, let's look at each of the three persons of the Trinity, beginning in this chapter with God the Father.

The Bible is clear that God is eternal. The first verse of Scripture is simple but profound: "In the beginning God created the heavens and the earth" (Genesis 1:1). God is the author of creation *in the beginning*. In other words, he was there before anything else existed. The Bible does not try to explain his eternal existence; it just presumes it.

The doctrine of God the Father is usually called "theology proper." *Theology* is a combination of two words: *theos*, which means "God," and *logos*, which means "word" or "study." Theology, in its broadest form, is the study of all Christian beliefs. So we use the phrase "theology proper" to refer to the specific study of God the Father.

This brief chapter cannot do justice to a study of God the Father. Indeed, volumes have been written on the topic and are still far from complete. For centuries, one approach to the study of God the Father has been looking at his attributes. We will thus look at some of his attributes, particularly those that have been commonly taught in churches and schools throughout history.

GOD IS LOVE

On the surface, this attribute of God is easy to understand. Most everyone has some understanding of the word *love*— even though the concept of love, especially God's love, is really much deeper and richer than we can grasp.

I was recently having a conversation with a hair stylist who is not a Christian. Somehow we got on the topic of God's love. When I tried to explain the nature of God's love, she exclaimed, "God could never love me like that!" From her perspective, she had "messed up" too many times. She thought she was both undeserving and unforgivable.

God by his very nature is love. John writes, "Anyone who does not love does not know God, *for God is love*" (1 John 4:8, italics added). Not only is God love by his nature, but he also demonstrates that love to us in numerous ways. His most profound act of love was sacrificing his Son, Jesus, for our sins: "God showed how much he loved us by sending his one and only Son into the world so that we might have eternal life through him. This is real love—not that we loved God, but that he loved us and sent his Son as a sacrifice to take away our sins" (1 John 4:9-10).

God loves his children now and through eternity. Because he gave us such an undeserved and unconditional love, we can love others as well. In fact, Jesus told us that loving God and others is the summation of our expected response to God:

> "'You must love the LORD your God with all your heart, all your soul, and all your mind.' This is the first and greatest commandment. A second is equally important: 'Love your neighbor as yourself.' The entire law and all the demands of the prophets are based on these two commandments."
>
> MATTHEW 22:37-40

GOD IS OMNIPOTENT

Omnipotent is the combination of two words meaning "all" and "powerful." God is able to do anything. In a poignant prayer, the prophet Jeremiah begins with these words: "O Sovereign LORD! You made the heavens and earth by your strong hand and powerful arm. Nothing is too hard for you!" (Jeremiah 32:17). In the early part of the prayer, Jeremiah acknowledges that God is in total control; he is sovereign. He affirms that God is the Creator of all things. Jeremiah prays because nothing is too hard for God to accomplish.

The apostle Paul reminds us in Ephesians 3:20 that God has the awesome power to accomplish anything through us: "Now all glory to God, who is able, through his mighty power at work within us, to accomplish infinitely more than we might ask or think."

But God will not use his omnipotence in ways that would be contrary to his nature and character. God will not lie or sin: "This truth gives them confidence that they have eternal life, which God—who does not lie—promised them before the world began" (Titus 1:2). God will neither tempt nor be tempted: "Remember, when you are being tempted, do not say, 'God is tempting me.' God is never tempted to do wrong, and he never tempts anyone else" (James 1:13). And God cannot deny himself: "If we are unfaithful, he remains faithful, for he cannot deny who he is" (2 Timothy 2:13).

GOD IS OMNISCIENT

Omniscient means "all knowing." God knows all because he is all, he created all, and all is subject to him. The apostle John affirms God's omniscience without equivocation in his first letter: "Even if we feel guilty, God is greater than our feelings, and *he knows everything*" (1 John 3:20, italics added).

God is never caught by surprise. He knows us far better than we know ourselves. He is fully aware of everything all the time. Nothing is hidden from him. He knows all the details of everything in time and everything in eternity. We can have great confidence in God because he both knows everything and can do anything. Not one of our needs, pains, questions, hopes, or dreams is beyond his scope.

GOD IS OMNIPRESENT

Omnipresent means "present everywhere." God is not bound by space or time. Many centuries ago, King David acknowledged this attribute of God in Psalm 139, a majestic prayer encompassing all three of God's *omni* characteristics: "I can never escape from your Spirit! I can never get away from your presence! If I go up to heaven, you are there; if I go down to the grave, you are there. If I ride the wings of the morning, if I dwell by the farthest oceans, even there your hand will guide me, and your strength will support me" (verses 7-10).

GOD IS HOLY

I spent my early childhood years in church before dropping out in adolescence. And it is amazing to me how my formative years in church affected my spiritual development—indeed, my overall development. For example, I still remember the most frequent hymn we sang and that it was #1 in the hymnal.

That hymn was "Holy, Holy, Holy! Lord God Almighty." Originally composed in 1826, this classic hymn had a profound effect on my view of God. The first line of the hymn is a repetition of the title: "Holy, Holy, Holy! Lord God Almighty."

At the time, I didn't understand what "holy" meant, but I sensed it was something special about God. Though our church was anything but lively, I could see the faces of the adults come alive when they sang these words. Without a doubt, I knew God was holy.

I would later learn that *holy* often means "set apart"—in God's case, totally set apart from sin. *Holy* is also used in the Bible to mean that God is totally worthy of our devotion.

Note the psalmist's words in Psalm 99:9: "Exalt the LORD our God, and worship at his holy mountain in Jerusalem, for the LORD our God is holy!" We exalt God because he is holy. We worship God because he is holy.

It is God's attribute of holiness that he desires we imitate: "You must be holy because I, the LORD your God, am holy" (Leviticus 19:2). Of course, we cannot be sinless and holy as God is, but we should strive in God's power to move closer and closer to holiness. Through God's power, we should "work at living in peace with everyone, and work at living a holy life, for those who are not holy will not see the Lord" (Hebrews 12:14).

GOD IS GOOD

My father used to wonder why we sometimes referred to people as "good men" or "good women." From his perspective, really no one apart from God was good. Of course, we use the word *good* somewhat loosely today, referring more to the general character of a person. We fully realize that no person is perfectly good. "Only God is truly good" (Luke 18:19).

What are the implications of God's goodness for believers? For one, it means he forgives us unconditionally. We can never sin beyond the forgiveness of God. He sent his Son to die for our sins so that his goodness can become our goodness.

Another implication of God's goodness is his grace. Not only is our forgiveness undeserved, but every good gift we receive is undeserved. Through his goodness and grace, God gives to us abundantly when we deserve nothing.

God's goodness also means we receive his comfort and mercy when we are hurt and suffering. Therefore, "let us come boldly to the throne of our gracious God. There we will receive his mercy, and we will find grace to help us when we need it most" (Hebrews 4:16).

God's goodness is not some esoteric theological concept that few understand. It is a clear and powerful description of his nature. It is a tangible reality that touches our lives in our times of need. God demonstrates his compassion for us through his goodness.

Think of one of the lowest moments in your life. For me, it was the death of my dad when I was a young man. Perhaps even more, I felt intense grief and pain decades later when one of my grandsons died. Though I will never get over these deaths, I did get through them. God, in his goodness, showered his compassion on me and gave me his comfort. Such is the reason I can affirm with Paul: "All praise to God, the Father of our Lord Jesus Christ. God is our merciful Father and the source of all comfort" (2 Corinthians 1:3).

God is indeed good. He is good all the time.

GOD IS RIGHTEOUS

I still remember the time I found myself caught in a family's feud over an estate. Of the four adult children, two were adamant that their parents had promised them more than the will stated. Of course, the will was final and binding.

One of the more vocal protests came from an adult daughter who had cared for her dying mother the last seven months of her life. She exclaimed, "I took care of her! I deserve more!"

Much of our culture today is a culture of entitlement. We think we deserve things, and *more* of those things. The image of following Christ, however, is one of serving and a willingness to be last. Paul's picture of Christ is powerful: "Though he was God, he did not think of equality with God as something to cling to. Instead, he gave up his divine privileges; he took the humble position of a slave and was born as a human being. When he appeared in human form, he humbled himself in obedience to God and died a criminal's death on a cross" (Philippians 2:6-8).

That's not exactly an entitlement mentality.

What is our entitlement as humans? We have none. We deserve nothing good. We have no righteousness of our own. From a biblical perspective, *righteousness* means we are "made right" with God. But the Bible teaches that our own righteousness is "nothing but filthy rags" (Isaiah 64:6).

What we *deserve* is eternal separation from God. That's the bad news. The good news is that we can be made righteous. We can have the filth of our sins taken away by the righteousness of God. "For God made Christ, who never sinned, to be the offering for our sin, so that we could be made right with God through Christ" (2 Corinthians 5:21).

God is perfect. He is total righteousness. We are totally imperfect and unrighteous. But for those who believe that Jesus died for our sins, we can be made right in God's eyes.

We can dwell in heaven with him because our sins have been taken away.

That is the nature of God's righteousness. And that is the good news for you and me.

※

DISCUSSION QUESTIONS

1. Give a quick explanation of the three "omni" words: *omnipotence*, *omniscience*, and *omnipresence*.

2. What does *holy* mean as an attribute of God? What does it mean that we should strive to be holy since we are not God?

3. How is righteousness the opposite of entitlement?

I BELIEVE IN GOD THE SON

In the course of a particular day, I heard the name Jesus expressed three different ways. The first time was at an office where a man, looking intently at his mobile phone, hit a chair with his knee. He cried out, "Oh, Jesus." I doubt he was thinking anything holy at that moment.

The second instance was the reporting of a survey by a polling firm. Basically, the poll was one of religious preferences. "Jesus" was one of many choices—much like he is viewed in culture today.

In the third example, I was watching a YouTube video in which the speaker was talking about how Jesus had changed her life. Her words and tone were reverent and inspiring.

It is rare that someone has not ever heard the name of

Jesus today. How they understand the meaning is varied. How they respond to the name varies as well. We know, however, that everyone will be called to respond to the name of Jesus at some point. And everyone will respond in reverence and awe. The apostle Paul writes, "Therefore, God elevated him to the place of highest honor and gave him the name above all other names, that at the name of Jesus every knee should bow, in heaven and on earth and under the earth, and every tongue declare that Jesus Christ is Lord, to the glory of God the Father" (Philippians 2:9-11).

The greatest demonstration of God's love was his sending Jesus to us. God came into the physical world. God came into the realm of humanity. Jesus was both fully God and fully man. Such a concept can be hard to grasp since it can only happen by the miraculous hand of God. Yet it happened. And that one person changed the course of history forever.

JESUS IS FULLY HUMAN

The doctrine of the virgin birth of Jesus is a crucial part of the doctrine of his full humanity. In Matthew 1:18 we read this truth clearly: "This is how Jesus the Messiah was born. His mother, Mary, was engaged to be married to Joseph. But before the marriage took place, while she was still a virgin, she became pregnant through the power of the Holy Spirit."

This miraculous conception means that God is the Father of Jesus through the work of the Holy Spirit. But Jesus is also the son of Mary. He was fully God, and he was also fully human. His birth was the fulfillment of Isaiah 7:14, according to the Gospel of Matthew: "All of this occurred to fulfill the Lord's message through his prophet: 'Look! The virgin will conceive a child! She will give birth to a son, and they will call him Immanuel, which means "God is with us"'" (Matthew 1:22-23).

Other than sinning, Jesus demonstrated all the traits of humanity. For example, his body was weary. At one point, he was on a boat and slept through a storm: "Suddenly, a fierce storm struck the lake, with waves breaking into the boat. But Jesus was sleeping" (Matthew 8:24).

When Jesus went into the wilderness to fast, pray, and prepare for his earthly ministry, the long fast caused him to hunger, just like any human: "For forty days and forty nights he fasted and became very hungry" (Matthew 4:2).

Jesus also dealt with the full range of human emotions. He demonstrated anger at how people responded to the death of his friend Lazarus: "When Jesus saw [Mary, the sister of Lazarus] weeping and saw the other people wailing with her, a deep anger welled up within him, and he was deeply troubled" (John 11:33). Though his emotion of anger was directed at their unbelief, Jesus was also saddened by the death of Lazarus: "Then Jesus wept" (John 11:35).

Jesus became fully human to live the life we experience. But unlike ours, his life was sinless and perfect. He was perfectly obedient when no other person could be. Paul compares Jesus to Adam. The former was the perfect man. The latter was the man through whom sin entered the world: "Because one person disobeyed God, many became sinners. But because one other person obeyed God, many will be made righteous" (Romans 5:19).

Jesus understands us in all our humanity because he is fully human. He thus represents us perfectly before God: "It was necessary for him to be made in every respect like us, his brothers and sisters, so that he could be our merciful and faithful High Priest before God. Then he could offer a sacrifice that would take away the sins of the people" (Hebrews 2:17). Further, because Jesus "has gone through suffering and testing, he is able to help us when we are being tested" (Hebrews 2:18).

God loves us so much that he sent his Son to die for us. But Jesus first lived a life that was fully human, fully tempted, and full of struggles and pain. Indeed, the greatest sacrifice took place on the cross when he died for us. But he suffered and struggled in his life as well.

In many ways, Christ's sacrifice began at the moment of his birth. It would culminate in his death. But through it all, Jesus was fully human.

JESUS IS FULLY GOD

Yes, Jesus was born of Mary. Thus, he is fully human. But he was conceived by the power of the Holy Spirit, so he is also fully God.

The angels not only proclaimed the birth of the human baby named Jesus, they also proclaimed that God himself was coming into the world: "The Savior—yes, the Messiah, the Lord—has been born today in Bethlehem, the city of David!" (Luke 2:11). And, as we noted above from Matthew 1:23, Jesus was called *Immanuel*, which means "God is with us."

The apostle Paul writes, "God in all his fullness was pleased to live in Christ. . . . For in Christ lives all the fullness of God in a human body" (Colossians 1:19; 2:9). We sometimes say that Jesus is "God incarnate," which means "God in the flesh."

We can learn a lot about Jesus in his encounters with those who opposed him, particularly the Pharisees. In a terse exchange with those austere religious leaders, Jesus began to reveal his identity as not only a man, but also as God. He told them that if they really knew the Father, they would know him as well: "Since you don't know who I am, you don't know who my Father is. If you knew me, you would also know my Father" (John 8:19).

The pinnacle of the exchange came when Jesus claimed

the name "I Am." His words were aimed directly at the Pharisees: "I tell you the truth, before Abraham was even born, I Am!" (John 8:58). Jesus assumed the same title God had taken for himself in Exodus 3:14 when he spoke to Moses: "I Am Who I Am. Say this to the people of Israel: I Am has sent me to you."

The Pharisees clearly knew that Jesus was claiming to be God. They were ready to stone him to death for heresy: "At that point they picked up stones to throw at him. But Jesus was hidden from them and left the Temple" (John 8:59).

The deity of Jesus can also be understood in the offices he held: prophet, priest, and king. God often spoke through the prophets to the people. Moses told the people of Israel that other prophets like him would rise up: "The Lord your God will raise up for you a prophet like me from among your fellow Israelites. You must listen to him" (Deuteronomy 18:15). The Lord then confirmed Moses' words: "I will raise up a prophet like you from among their fellow Israelites. I will put my words in his mouth, and he will tell the people everything I command him" (Deuteronomy 18:18).

When the apostle Peter preached in the formative days of the early church, he affirmed that Christ was the fulfillment of all prophecy and the perfect prophet to speak for God: "Anyone who will not listen to that Prophet will be completely cut off from God's people" (Acts 3:23).

In the Old Testament, when Abram (Abraham) saw the

priest Melchizedek, he recognized him as someone to be revered. When Abraham returned from a military victory, he was met by Melchizedek with bread and wine (Genesis 14:18-22). Melchizedek is identified as "the king of Salem and a priest of God Most High." Melchizedek blessed Abraham, who in turn gave the priest a tenth of what he had recovered in battle.

Though Melchizedek remains a somewhat mysterious person in Scripture, we do recognize him as a priest of God. Christ has entered through the curtain into God's inner sanctuary to be our high priest in the lineage of Melchizedek. As Hebrews 6:20 notes, "Jesus has already gone in there for us. He has become our eternal High Priest in the order of Melchizedek."

We now have the perfect High Priest, Jesus, interceding for us constantly. Only a priest who is truly God could make this intercession. In his perfection, Jesus intercedes for our sin before God.

Christ also holds the office of king. Numerous prophecies in the Old Testament point to the coming king. For example, the psalmist writes in Psalm 2:6-7, "The Lord declares, 'I have placed my chosen king on the throne in Jerusalem, on my holy mountain.' The king proclaims the Lord's decree: 'The Lord said to me, "You are my son. Today I have become your Father."'"

The New Testament also affirms the kingship of Jesus,

both in his early earthly life and in his death on the cross. The traveling wise men asked the question regarding the birth of Jesus: "Where is the newborn king of the Jews? We saw his star as it rose, and we have come to worship him" (Matthew 2:2). As the soldiers stripped and beat Jesus shortly before they nailed him to the cross, "they knelt before him in mockery and taunted, 'Hail! King of the Jews!' And they spit on him and grabbed the stick and struck him on the head with it" (Matthew 27:29-30).

From birth to death, whether in adoration or scorn, those around Jesus were keenly aware that he was a king; or, at the very least, that he claimed to be a king.

THE PRESENT MINISTRY OF CHRIST

Christ is building his church today. When the church first began in Jerusalem, it was Christ who was adding people to the congregation: "Each day the Lord added to their fellowship those who were being saved" (Acts 2:47). Indeed, the church is called "the body of Christ" (1 Corinthians 12:12), a clear proclamation that Jesus is leading the church even today.

Jesus is also praying for us who are believers. In my lifetime, I have been blessed to have many people pray for me, including some who prayed for me daily. In a church where I served as pastor, one lady enlisted more than one hundred other church members to join her in praying for me every day at noon. Regardless of their location or what they were doing, these church members would stop at noon and offer a brief prayer for me. It was both humbling and amazing.

What is even more humbling and amazing is that Jesus prays for every believer: "Therefore he is able, once and forever, to save those who come to God through him. He lives forever to intercede with God on their behalf" (Hebrews 7:25).

Jesus did not merely come to earth as a man who lived for three decades; he continues to minister to our churches and to us personally today. It is both exciting and assuring to know he is with us at this very moment. And it is with great expectation that we anticipate his future return.

THE FUTURE MINISTRY OF CHRIST

Jesus promised that one day he will return personally and visibly in glory to the earth; the dead will be raised; and Christ will judge all people in righteousness. Believers in Jesus will receive their resurrected and glorified bodies. They will also receive their reward and dwell forever in heaven with the Lord.

Christ was taken from his earthly ministry to his present ministry in heaven through the Ascension, the term we use to refer to that moment when he left earth and rose into the sky. The believers who witnessed this event were told to be encouraged because Jesus would return again:

After saying this, he was taken up into a cloud while they were watching, and they could no longer see him. As they strained to see him rising into heaven, two white-robed men suddenly stood among them. "Men of Galilee," they said, "why are you standing here staring into heaven? Jesus has been taken from you into heaven, but someday he will return from heaven in the same way you saw him go!"

ACTS 1:9-11

So, the story of Jesus continues, with the next anticipated event being his return. We wait both patiently and expectantly.

"He who is the faithful witness to all these things says, 'Yes, I am coming soon!' Amen! Come, Lord Jesus!" (Revelation 22:20).

DISCUSSION QUESTIONS

1. What is a clear example from the Bible that Jesus was fully human?

2. Why did Jesus come to earth as a man?

3. What does it mean to you that Jesus is praying for you regularly?

4

I BELIEVE IN GOD
THE HOLY SPIRIT

For most of my years in churches, I have heard little taught or preached on the Holy Spirit. While I heard such phrases as "one God, three persons," I heard very few sermons or read very few lessons that dealt with the person, role, and work of the Holy Spirit. There was a lot of teaching on God the Father. And we certainly learned much about God the Son. But we heard little to nothing about God the Holy Spirit.

In my twenties, I met a Christian man who was a member of what he described as "a Spirit-filled church." There is absolutely nothing wrong with this description. I wish all churches were truly led by the Holy Spirit. But when I visited his church, I heard some teaching about the Holy Spirit that I couldn't find in the Bible. I was confused!

I am in a church today that is biblically balanced in its teachings and understanding of the Holy Spirit. It is not like most churches I've been a part of, where teaching about the Holy Spirit was largely absent. But it's also not like some other churches that teach aspects of the Spirit that are not in Scripture.

We started this book with the chapter "I Believe in the Bible." The placement of that chapter is not incidental. We must check everything we hear and learn about God by using the Word of God, the Bible. That's true for *any* doctrine, and it's true for understanding the doctrine of the Holy Spirit. Let's see, then, what the Bible says about the Holy Spirit.

THE HOLY SPIRIT IS A PERSON

We will look at the Trinity as a whole in the next chapter. The doctrine of the Trinity, of course, is that God is one and exists in three persons. Most of us can understand the person of Jesus Christ. After all, we have good accounts of his life on earth in the four Gospels: Matthew, Mark, Luke, and John. As we noted in the previous chapter, Jesus was not only fully God, but he was fully man. We see his humanity throughout the Gospels.

For some, understanding God the Father as a person may not be as clear. The image of a father is different for different people, often depending on their relationship with their earthly father. Yet, for others, any concept of God may seem distant, especially for those who are not Christians.

But the very name of the Holy Spirit may cause us to pause as we consider him as a person. When we hear the word *spirit*, we might not grasp that the Spirit can be a person. We are more likely to think of a person as someone with humanlike qualities, as someone we can see or touch.

Yet the Holy Spirit is a person, not a mere influence. Paul writes in Ephesians 4:30, "Do not bring sorrow to God's Holy Spirit by the way you live. Remember, he has identified you as his own, guaranteeing that you will be saved on the day of redemption." As a person, the Holy Spirit can feel sorrow. Some translations, such as the NIV, ESV, and NJKV, say, "Do not grieve the Holy Spirit." The Holy Spirit is a person with real emotions, who feels emotional pain.

One way that we can respond to the Holy Spirit is by obeying what he tells us to do. In Acts 10:9-20, Peter receives a vision of clean and unclean animals. As Peter is trying to understand the vision, the Holy Spirit tells him that three men have come to see him: "Get up, go downstairs, and go with them without hesitation. Don't worry, for I have sent them" (Acts 10:20). The Holy Spirit gives Peter three brief commands, and Peter obeys. He wasn't obeying some unknown force; he was obeying the person of the Holy Spirit.

Through that encounter, God reveals the meaning of the vision to Peter. He tells Peter he should not view the Gentiles as unclean. After all, God shows no favoritism among groups. This vision soon leads to Peter preaching the gospel to all people, including those who were not Jews.

The Holy Spirit can also be lied to. For example, in another passage involving Peter, the apostle confronts Ananias and Sapphira for lying about their gifts to the church. Peter asserts that they have lied to *someone*, not a mere force or object. He confronts Ananias first in Acts 5:3: "Ananias, why have you let Satan fill your heart? You lied to the Holy Spirit, and you kept some of the money for yourself."

Three hours later, Peter confronts Ananias's wife, Sapphira: "How could the two of you even think of conspiring to test the Spirit of the Lord like this?" (Acts 5:9).

The Holy Spirit can be grieved. The Holy Spirit can be obeyed. The Holy Spirit can be the recipient of attempted deception. These are traits of someone with a personality. These are just a few of the examples where the Bible clearly teaches that the Holy Spirit is a person.

THE WORK OF THE HOLY SPIRIT IN THE BIBLE

The Father, Son, and Holy Spirit have always existed. All three persons were involved in Creation. For example, Genesis 1:26 says, "Then God said, 'Let us make human beings in our image, to be like us.'" In Genesis 1:2, the work of the Holy Spirit in Creation is described: "The earth was formless and empty, and darkness covered the deep waters. And the Spirit of God was hovering over the surface of the waters."

The Holy Spirit also teaches. Jesus taught his disciples, but the Holy Spirit teaches all believers. Jesus said, "When the Father sends the Advocate as my representative—that is, the Holy Spirit—he will teach you everything and will remind you of everything I have told you" (John 14:26).

Let that verse sink in for a moment. Have you ever wished you could have Jesus sit down with you and teach you his truths? What would it be like to hear directly from the Master? Well, that is the essence of what Jesus is saying in this verse. He taught his disciples directly. He often spoke and taught to the crowds as well. But the third person of the Trinity, the Holy Spirit, teaches *all* believers.

When you read your Bible and seek to hear from God, the Holy Spirit will give you clarity and understanding. Though we don't minimize the value of formal ministry and theological training, the Holy Spirit is there for all believers. He becomes your first teacher.

The Holy Spirit also prays for you to God the Father. Romans 8:26 is a powerful statement: "The Holy Spirit helps us in our weakness. For example, we don't know what God wants us to pray for. But the Holy Spirit prays for us with groanings that cannot be expressed in words."

My father died when I was still in my twenties. We were

very close. Indeed, he was not only my dad, but he was also my best friend. I prayed and prayed for God to heal him of his cancer. But with each passing day, Dad worsened. I admit I had trouble praying. I reached a point where I didn't even know how or what to pray.

Then I read Romans 8:26. The Holy Spirit used that verse to remind me that he was praying for me even when I could not pray myself. It was an incredible moment when again I got a taste of God's love for me.

The Holy Spirit also convicts us of sin. In John 16:8, Jesus states clearly that this would be part of the Holy Spirit's role: "When he [the Holy Spirit] comes, he will convict the world of its sin, and of God's righteousness, and of the coming judgment." When we read God's Word, we clearly see sin and its consequences. We know when we are being disobedient to Scripture. The Holy Spirit will also convict us of sin even when we don't have the Bible right in front of us. This role of the Spirit is critical for us to grow as believers in Christ.

Another work of the Holy Spirit is to help believers in many other ways. Jesus says in John 14:16, "I will ask the Father, and he will give you another Advocate, who will never leave you."

The word *Advocate* (NLT) is also translated as *Helper* (ESV), *Comforter* (KJV), and *Counselor* (CSB). You can see the similarities between the translations. The Holy Spirit is present to walk alongside us.

Indeed, the Greek word for *advocate* is *parakleton*, which is a combination of two words meaning "called" and "alongside." So the literal meaning of the work of the Holy Spirit is his call to work alongside believers. This truth is both powerful and encouraging. We have the third person of the Trinity, the Holy Spirit, who is walking with us. Also, note how John 14:16 concludes: "He will give you another Advocate, *who will never leave you*" (italics added). Not only is the Holy Spirit present to help us, but he is present to help us *at all times*.

You have likely heard the phrase "born again." It is a thoroughly biblical phrase articulated by Jesus and others. In John 3, when Jesus is speaking to Nicodemus, he says, "I tell you the truth, unless you are born again, you cannot see the Kingdom of God" (John 3:3).

Nicodemus is perplexed by these words, so Jesus provides further explanation:

> Humans can reproduce only human life, but the Holy Spirit gives birth to spiritual life. So don't be surprised when I say, "You must be born again." The wind blows wherever it wants. Just as you can hear the wind but can't tell where it comes from or

where it is going, so you can't explain how people
are born of the Spirit.
JOHN 3:6-8

Here, Jesus explains one of the key works of the Holy
Spirit: to give spiritual life to believers. All humans have
physical life, but only believers have spiritual life in Christ.
Jesus also makes it clear that we can't fully understand all that
the Spirit does.

In the Old Testament, the presence of the Spirit was selec-
tive and temporary. In the New Testament, his presence is
permanent and for all believers. Jesus said,

I will ask the Father, and he will give you another
Advocate, who will never leave you. He is the Holy
Spirit, who leads into all truth. The world cannot
receive him, because it isn't looking for him and
doesn't recognize him. But you know him, because
he lives with you now and later will be in you.
JOHN 14:16-17

The Holy Spirit indeed came to dwell in all believers
permanently, beginning with the birth of the church at
Pentecost (Acts 2:1-4). At the conclusion of Peter's sermon
at Pentecost, he invited all who have been called of God (Acts
2:39) to "receive the gift of the Holy Spirit" (Acts 2:38). The

Spirit began his work of regenerating, or giving new life to, believers. He continues that work in believers' lives today.

DISCUSSION QUESTIONS

1. Explain how the Bible teaches clearly that the Holy Spirit is a person.

2. What does it mean for us today that the Holy Spirit is our Advocate?

3. How can the Holy Spirit teach you and convict you today?

5

I BELIEVE IN THE TRINITY

I have a first name, a middle name, and a last name. But God doesn't have three names like I do. God is three persons. Each person is unique and is identified in the Bible: Father, Son, and Holy Spirit. God has eternally existed as three persons, but there is only one God.

In the previous three chapters, we looked at each of the three persons of the Trinity individually. In this brief summary, we will look at the persons of the Godhead in the context of the doctrine of the Trinity.

The concept of three persons in one God is difficult to grasp with our finite minds. We call it the doctrine of the Trinity, but the word *Trinity* cannot be found in Scripture.

Still, it is abundantly clear in the Bible that God is one, and that God is three persons.

In describing the act of creation, Genesis uses the plural (three persons) and the singular (one God) to describe God. In Genesis 1:26, for example, "God said, 'Let us make human beings in our image, to be like us.'" God is obviously referring to more than one person with the use of *us* and *our*. Then, in Genesis 1:27, God is singular with the use of the pronouns *his* and *he*: "So God created human beings in his own image. In the image of God he created them; male and female he created them."

A powerful and clear picture of the Trinity takes place in the baptism of Jesus by John the Baptist:

> After his baptism, as Jesus came up out of the water,
> the heavens were opened, and he saw the Spirit of
> God descending like a dove and settling on him.
> And a voice from heaven said, "This is my dearly
> loved Son, who brings me great joy."
> MATTHEW 3:16-17

God the Son was baptized. God the Holy Spirit came upon Jesus. And God the Father spoke.

One of the passages commonly referred to as "the Great Commission" presents the Trinity as well. Jesus speaks these words: "Go and make disciples of all the nations, baptizing them in the name of the Father and the Son and the Holy Spirit" (Matthew 28:19). When we are baptized and confess our identity as believers, we do so in the name of all three persons of the Trinity.

We are also taught that our salvation is the work of the Trinity:

> He brought this Good News of peace to you
> Gentiles who were far away from him, and peace
> to the Jews who were near. Now all of us can come
> to the Father through the same Holy Spirit because
> of what Christ has done for us.
>
> EPHESIANS 2:17-18

ONE GOD

Even as we affirm that God is three persons, we must also affirm that he is *one*. When God was preparing Israel to enter the Promised Land, he exhorted them to obey all the commands of the God who is one: "Listen, O Israel! The LORD is our God, the LORD alone" (Deuteronomy 6:4). Some translations, such as the NIV, use *one* to identify "the LORD alone": "Hear, O Israel: The LORD our God, the LORD is one."

In his letter to the Romans, Paul asserts, "There is only one God, and he makes people right with himself only by faith, whether they are Jews or Gentiles" (Romans 3:30). And

James reminds us that even the demons recognize that there is but one God: "You say you have faith, for you believe that there is one God. Good for you! Even the demons believe this, and they tremble in terror" (James 2:19).

THREE PERSONS

We use the word *person* in our common vernacular to refer to individual people. We thus might confuse the concept of God as three persons when we think of him in human terms. For example, if we refer to Rebecca, Jim, and Sheila, we are referring to three distinct people who are different beings. But when we refer to the Father, Son, and Holy Spirit, we are referring to one God of the same essence, not three. God relates to himself in three persons even though he is one.

Throughout Scripture, all three persons of the Trinity are referred to as God. God the Father is a person of the Trinity. Jesus himself taught his disciples and us to pray to the Father: "Pray like this: Our Father in heaven, may your name be kept holy" (Matthew 6:9). Two realities are evident in this passage. First, God the Father is in his heavenly abode. Second, because the Son is praying to the Father, God the Father and God the Son are different persons.

God the Son is a person of the Trinity. As Paul explains, "In Christ lives all the fullness of God in a human body"

(Colossians 2:9). This verse not only demonstrates that Christ is fully God, but it is also a powerful reminder that he is fully human as well.

God the Holy Spirit is the third person of the Trinity and is always referred to with the personal pronoun *he*. In Ephesians 4:30, Paul writes, "Do not bring sorrow to God's Holy Spirit by the way you live." The Holy Spirit is obviously a person because you cannot grieve an inanimate object or a mere force. The Holy Spirit is obviously a person of the Trinity because he is *God's* Holy Spirit.

THE IMPLICATIONS OF THE DOCTRINE OF THE TRINITY

Though we confess that we are not fully knowledgeable about all the specifics of the doctrine of the Trinity, we can see practical implications that emanate from this doctrine.

First, Christianity is the only belief that affirms the Trinity. This makes it unique among world religions, including other monotheistic (one god) faiths. Imagine Christianity without the Father, the Son, or the Holy Spirit. You cannot fathom the Christian faith without all three persons because the Trinity captures the essence of Christianity.

Second, the Trinity demonstrates the incredible relational aspects of God. Jesus the Son submits to the Father. The Father loves the Son. The Son sends the Holy Spirit so that his presence will be in every believer. We ultimately understand the fullness of relational issues when we see the relationships within the Trinity.

Third, the Trinity helps us grasp the meaning of bringing glory to God. Some people struggle with God's desire to bring glory to himself because they fail to see the glory inherent in the Trinity's relationship among three persons. They perceive wrongly that this act of seeking glory is egotistical. But each person of the Trinity is bringing glory to the other in the relationships between the Father, the Son, and the Holy Spirit.

Fourth, the Trinity helps us understand the gospel more fully. "God so loved the world that he gave his one and only Son" (John 3:16, NIV). The Son died on the cross in obedience to the Father. Jesus demonstrated the agony of obedience in his prayer to the Father shortly before he went to the cross: "Father, if you are willing, please take this cup of suffering away from me. Yet I want your will to be done, not mine" (Luke 22:42). After the resurrection and ascension of Jesus, the Holy Spirit began to convict people of their sins and their need to embrace the gospel. The Great Commission is a Trinitarian mandate to evangelize, and we baptize in the name of the Trinity: "Therefore, go and make disciples of all the nations, baptizing them in the name of the Father and the Son and the Holy Spirit" (Matthew 28:19).

Finally, the Trinity is necessary for us to grow as Christians. As we noted, the three persons of the Trinity are all involved in evangelism and regeneration. It is the Holy Spirit who is particularly involved in our sanctification, meaning our spiritual growth as Christians. Paul writes, "I bring you the Good News so that I might present you as an acceptable offering to God, made holy by the Holy Spirit" (Romans 15:16). Such is the reason Christ said it would be better for him to leave the Holy Spirit with us.

God loves us. The Father sends the Son. The Son sacrifices his life for us and defeats death. The Son ascends to heaven and sends the Holy Spirit to dwell within believers. The Holy Spirit becomes our advocate and teacher that we might grow as believers.

THE CHALLENGES OF UNDERSTANDING THE TRINITY

I was in a study group where different members attempted to articulate their understanding of the Trinity. No one was a biblical beginner, but we all had trouble expressing the precise words that would best articulate the doctrine. One member said he had read several theological articles on the Trinity and came away confused with the complexity of the writings.

We must first admit that the doctrine of the Trinity is not easy for finite minds to grasp. As we noted earlier, the word *Trinity* cannot be found in Scripture. Thus we can jump to erroneous conclusions about a word with the *tri* prefix. But neither the word *Trinity* nor any human articulation can fully present the mysteries of this doctrine. We sometimes want to explain the eternal in ways that are finite and human-centered. Such is the reason we attempt to use analogies and illustrations for this doctrine. None is truly sufficient. Some are erroneous, even contrary to biblical teachings.

We are told in Scripture that we have only a partial view of the infinite and of the truths of God in our finite state. Paul said, "Now our knowledge is partial and incomplete, and even the gift of prophecy reveals only part of the whole picture!" (1 Corinthians 13:9). We who are creatures cannot fully grasp the complexities of the Creator. The doctrine of the Trinity is one of those critical truths we accept by faith.

Yet we cannot minimize the critical importance of the Trinity. For example, if Jesus is not fully God and a distinct person of the Trinity, he could not have taken our punishment for sins on the cross and risen from the dead. And if Jesus was not resurrected, we have a faith that is in vain. As Paul observes, "If Christ has not been raised, then your faith is useless and you are still guilty of your sins. In that case, all who have died believing in Christ are lost! And if our hope in Christ is only for this life, we are more to be pitied than anyone in the world" (1 Corinthians 15:17-19).

Though we may not be able to understand fully all the aspects of the doctrine of the Trinity, we can affirm that the Bible teaches clear truths about it. Each person of the

Trinity is fully God. We wrote of this truth in the previous three chapters. But the Bible also teaches that God is one and only one.

Yes, the doctrine of the Trinity can be a challenge. There are three distinct persons of the Trinity, and each has the whole being of God. Though we cannot fit these truths in the context of human-centered logic, we accept them by faith. With Paul we affirm, "Now we see things imperfectly, like puzzling reflections in a mirror, but then we will see everything with perfect clarity. All that I know now is partial and incomplete, but then I will know everything completely, just as God now knows me completely" (1 Corinthians 13:12).

We wait until we are with Christ to understand completely. Until then, we walk by faith and live by hope.

DISCUSSION QUESTIONS

1. Explain how the Great Commission passage of Matthew 28:19 highlights the critical roles of each person of the Trinity.

2. How does the Bible teach that salvation is a work of the Trinity?

3. What does 1 Corinthians 13:12 tell us, specifically as we try to grasp the doctrine of the Trinity?

6

I BELIEVE IN PRAYER

Because of the number of speaking opportunities I've had, I often have people ask me if I remember meeting them at a certain venue. I'm always embarrassed when I can't recall. It's not that I'm so important; I'm not. But after four decades, I've simply met too many people in too many places to keep track.

But I do remember one particular time and place.

The town wasn't very big. It was somewhere in central Arkansas. If I recall correctly, it had a small college or university.

My purpose in the visit was to preach for a missions emphasis in a church's worship services. This church had not been on my radar—but it should have been. For one thing, the church had experienced breakout growth for more than a decade, growth that defied the demographics of the community. But I knew of many other churches that were larger and some that had a faster growth rate. Still, I'm not sure if I could recall a church reaching as many people in a similar community.

The pastor had said he wanted me to "bless his church," but I was the one who received the blessing.

I learned the reason for the growth of the church. I learned why many people had become followers of Christ. I learned why many members had become missionaries. Yes, I learned why God was blessing this church.

It was prayer.

In fact, I can't recall ever seeing a prayer ministry in a church with this type of sustained emphasis and power. Allow me to explain.

Beginning in 2006 or 2007, members of the church had started praying around the clock—every hour of every day, and every day of every year. The prayer had gone on, uninterrupted, ever since. A church member, for example, volunteered to pray from 2:00 a.m. to 3:00 a.m. every Thursday morning for a year. When the hour was up, he or she called the person who was scheduled to pray from 3:00 a.m. to 4:00 a.m. for a quick handoff. This cycle of prayer has gone on unabated for more than fifteen years now.

The pastor told us he doesn't have to recruit volunteers to pray. In fact, church members must take turns joining the intercessory prayer ministry each year. The church provides guidance for the hour of prayer—with both general and specific prayer requests. Some members told me that the hour goes by quickly. They also said they've experienced some of their greatest spiritual growth during their involvement in the prayer ministry.

THE EARLY CHURCH AND PRAYER

I never cease to be amazed at the power of prayer when the church began in Jerusalem. After Jesus ascended into heaven, the disciples of Christ went to the upper room of the house where they were staying. And what did they do as they waited for what would take place next? "They all met together and were constantly united in prayer" (Acts 1:14).

Then it happened. The Holy Spirit came upon the believers. "Suddenly, there was a sound from heaven like the roaring of a mighty windstorm, and it filled the house where they were sitting" (Acts 2:2). Peter, filled with the Holy Spirit, preached to the crowd. Thousands became followers of Christ: "Those who believed what Peter said were baptized and added to the church that day—about 3,000 in all" (Acts 2:41).

The church was launched after a small group of believers "were constantly united in prayer" (Acts 1:14). Don't miss, however, what the new church did at its very beginning. "All the believers devoted themselves to the apostles' teaching, and to fellowship, and to sharing in meals (including the Lord's Supper), *and to prayer*" (Acts 2:42, italics added). One of the first priorities of the early church was prayer. It inaugurated the church. And it sustained the church.

It is important, then, to understand why prayer is so vital to the church.

WHY DO WE PRAY?

As we've discussed, God is omniscient, which means he knows everything. Indeed, he knows all of our needs, hurts, desires, and hopes before we ever articulate them in prayer. Jesus instructed his followers how to pray in what we commonly call the Lord's Prayer. The first Gospel records this prayer in Matthew 6:9-13. But Jesus prefaced his instructions with these words: "When you pray, don't babble on and on as the Gentiles do. They think their prayers are answered merely by repeating their words again and again. Don't be like them, for your Father knows exactly what you need even before you ask him!" (Matthew 6:7-8).

Jesus' words are powerfully instructive. First, we are reminded that the efficacy of prayer does not depend on our repetition or cadence as we speak to God. We are speaking as a child speaks to his or her father. The relationship is warm, familial, and informal.

Second, Jesus tells us that we can be confident that the

Father knows our prayers even before we articulate them. We don't pray because the Father needs information. We pray because God desires this relationship with us. Jesus reminds us to approach prayer as though we are talking to a loving father who wants the best for us: "You fathers—if your children ask for a fish, do you give them a snake instead? Or if they ask for an egg, do you give them a scorpion? Of course not! So if you sinful people know how to give good gifts to your children, how much more will your heavenly Father give the Holy Spirit to those who ask him" (Luke 11:11-13).

We pray because we want to acknowledge our dependence on a Father who loves us unconditionally. We pray because God not only listens but listens with concern and a willingness to respond to us. We pray because God delights in our relationship with him.

Further, we pray in order to align our lives with God's mission. We pray as Jesus modeled: "May your Kingdom come soon. May your will be done on earth, as it is in heaven" (Matthew 6:10). It is amazing that we have the opportunity to pray for the advancement of God's Kingdom and that we get to participate with the King in that mission.

DOES PRAYER WORK?

Jesus reminds us that the effectiveness of prayer begins simply with our willingness and desire to pray. "Keep on asking, and you will receive what you ask for. Keep on seeking, and you will find. Keep on knocking, and the door will be opened to you. For everyone who asks, receives. Everyone who seeks, finds. And to everyone who knocks, the door will be opened" (Matthew 7:7-8).

Of course, we should always ask according to God's will (Matthew 6:10), but that shouldn't preclude us from asking with boldness. Indeed, the biggest obstacle we face is not asking at all: "You don't have what you want because you don't ask God for it" (James 4:2).

I spoke recently with a man named Greg, who had prayed for days to be accepted into a prestigious graduate school. When the school did not accept him, he was devastated. He reluctantly started a business until he could decide what to do with his life. The business began to grow well beyond his expectations and even his desires. As the business grew, he was able to fund two ministries where he served in a volunteer capacity. Greg's generosity fueled the ministries to expand their outreach, footprint, and impact.

One of the ministries expanded into Florida. On a volunteer ministry trip to Florida, Greg met a lady who would later become his wife. They are now the parents of three children. Greg told me he is happier than he's ever been, and that his life is more fulfilled than he ever would have anticipated.

Then he shared the rest of the story.

"When I prayed to be accepted into grad school," he said, "I did so with the wrong motives. I was seeking prestige and power. I can tell you beyond a shadow of doubt I was not praying for God's will to be done. God was so good to answer my prayer with what was best for me, not with what I thought was best for me."

The apostle John writes succinctly and clearly: "We are confident that he hears us whenever we ask for anything that pleases him" (1 John 5:14). Greg learned a powerful lesson about praying according to the will of God—praying for the things that please God.

HOW DO WE APPROACH GOD IN PRAYER?

Hebrews 4:16 is a good reminder of how we should approach God in prayer: "Let us come boldly to the throne of our gracious God. There we will receive his mercy, and we will find grace to help us when we need it most."

We are to approach God with confidence. He is our heavenly Father, and he wants what is best for us. This confidence is also reflected in 1 John 5:15: "Since we know he hears us when we make our requests, we also know that he will give us what we ask for."

We also must approach God in prayer with clean hearts. But we know that we are sinners in need of forgiveness. Such is the reason we confess our sins as a beginning to our prayers. The psalmist says, "If I had not confessed the sin in my heart, the Lord would not have listened" (Psalm 66:18).

It has been popular for many years to use the acronym ACTS as a guide for our prayers. We first *adore* God and praise him. We enter into an act of worship as we begin to pray. Then we *confess* our sins so that we come to God with pure hearts. The next act of prayer is *thanksgiving*. We spend a healthy portion of our prayer time praising God for who he is and what he has done. We praise him for answered prayers as well. Finally, we enter into a time of *supplication*—asking God for specific needs for others and for ourselves.

I would not enter into a biblical debate with someone who uses the ACTS guide for their prayer life. I would simply be grateful they are so faithful in prayer. But my understanding of the doctrine of prayer is that the *C* should come first. We must confess our sins so our hearts can be pure for adoration, thanksgiving, and supplication. We affirm the promise of 1 John 1:9: "If we confess our sins to him, he is faithful and just to forgive us our sins and to cleanse us from all wickedness."

Ultimately, we approach God with complete humility because he is God and we are not. He is the Creator; we are the creation. Indeed, we approach him with a posture of total humility and lack of pride because "God opposes the proud but gives grace to the humble" (James 4:6).

Indeed, when we come to God with total humility, we

are not only coming close to him, but that act of humility is also an act to resist the devil: "Humble yourselves before God. Resist the devil, and he will flee from you" (James 4:7).

The doctrine of prayer intersects with the doctrine of the Trinity. For example, God the Father hears our prayers. God the Son taught us to pray. And God the Holy Spirit intercedes for us in prayer.

Sometimes we think of the word *doctrine* as an intellectual belief in a biblical truth. For certain, it is that, but it is much more. We must have our personal doctrine of prayer that moves us from self-dependence to total and humble dependence on God. We must be men and women totally devoted to God in prayer. Only then will we fully understand this amazing relationship we can have with God, who loves us completely and unconditionally.

DISCUSSION QUESTIONS

1. What do you think it means in Acts 2:42 that all the believers devoted themselves to prayer?

2. Explain Matthew 7:7 and how it should relate to your personal prayer life.

3. Why is confession of sins vital in our prayers?

7

I BELIEVE IN ANGELS, DEMONS, AND SATAN

When I start each chapter with "I believe," you might assume I am making a statement of advocacy for the subject of the chapter. That is certainly the case in all the other chapters. In this chapter, however, when I speak of demons and Satan, my "belief" statement is one of simply affirming their reality. Indeed, it is critically important for us to believe in the existence of these beings. And it is likewise important for us to understand them from the biblical perspective.

The danger lies in the extremes. On the one hand, we can expand the concept of angels, demons, and Satan far beyond their biblical reality. The combination of cultural influence and biblical illiteracy certainly has influenced many people,

Christians included, to view these largely unseen beings as something more than they are.

On the other hand, we can ignore their reality at our peril. These supernatural beings really exist. They really have power. They really are at work in our world today. We cannot resist demons and Satan if we don't believe they exist.

ANGELS

Perhaps one of the most common points of confusion regarding angels is how they relate to humans. Many people believe that humans become angels when they die, that they get their "angel wings." This belief does not match the biblical teachings about angels.

Angels are unique beings created by God. They are spiritual creatures. They do not have bodies like humans. Angels are, for the most part, unseen, but there are times in Scripture where God allows them to be seen. They are highly intelligent beings with unique powers. They are described in Scripture as "far greater in power and strength" than "proud and arrogant" people (2 Peter 2:10, 11).

What are the roles of angels? As we will see in the discussion of demons in this chapter, angels are involved in spiritual warfare against the demons and Satan. When the king of Aram sent his troops to seize Elisha, a massive army appeared ready to capture the prophet. In fact, Elisha's servant began to panic: "Oh, sir, what will we do now?" (2 Kings 6:15).

Elisha knew that God's angels were there for the battle, but he wanted his servant to see them as well. He told the servant not to be afraid because "there are more on our side than on theirs!" (2 Kings 6:16). And though angels are not typically visible, Elisha prayed that his servant would see the army on the hillside: "'O LORD, open his eyes and let him see!' The LORD opened the young man's eyes, and when he looked up, he saw that the hillside around Elisha was filled with horses and chariots of fire" (2 Kings 6:17).

Angels were also created to praise God and worship him. The record of angels worshiping God is particularly powerful in the book of Revelation: "Each of these living beings had six wings, and their wings were covered all over with eyes, inside and out. Day after day and night after night they keep on saying, 'Holy, holy, holy is the Lord God, the Almighty— the one who always was, who is, and who is still to come'" (Revelation 4:8).

Aggelos, the Greek word from which we get our word *angel*, simply means "messenger." And this describes another role that angels play. They are sent by God to give messages to humans. Some of those messages were major announcements, such as the coming of Jesus into the world. God sent the angel Gabriel to Mary to let her know that she would be carrying the Christ child:

> "Don't be afraid, Mary," the angel told her, "for you have found favor with God! You will conceive and give birth to a son, and you will name him Jesus. He will be very great and will be called the Son of the Most High. The Lord God will give him the throne of his ancestor David. And he will reign over Israel forever; his Kingdom will never end!"
>
> LUKE 1:30-33

God also created angels to protect humans: "He will order his angels to protect you wherever you go" (Psalm 91:11). Hebrews 1:14 likewise reminds us, "Angels are only servants—spirits sent to care for people who will inherit salvation."

There seems to be a hierarchy of angels. In Jude 1:9, Michael is referred to as "one of the mightiest of the angels." Likewise, Michael is seen leading other angels in spiritual warfare: "Then there was war in heaven. Michael and his angels fought against the dragon and his angels" (Revelation 12:7). The dragon specifically refers to Satan (Revelation 12:9), so Michael was leading the fight against the leader of the fallen angels that are also called *demons*.

There have been various attempts to describe an explicit

order of angels. Often included in the hierarchy are the *cherubim*, who are mentioned more than ninety times in the Bible, and the *seraphim*, who are mentioned only in Isaiah 6. The Bible, however, does not provide any details about a ranking of angels, and any attempt to create a hierarchy is only speculation.

DEMONS

Frankly, many Christians today get their perspective on demons from movies and books. Indeed, an entire genre has emerged over the past several decades. On the one hand, the popular depiction gets it right by demonstrating the existence of demons. On the other hand, some of the depictions are entirely unbiblical.

Demons are fallen angels who sinned against God. They are evil, and they seek to perpetuate evil in the world today. As noted above, they can be called angels, but always in a context that makes it clear they are fallen angels (e.g., "the dragon and his angels" in Revelation 12:7).

Though some have speculated to determine the exact point in history when the fallen angels rebelled, the Bible doesn't offer that specificity. We do know, however, that these fallen angels have already been judged by God: "God did not spare even the angels who sinned. He threw them into hell, in gloomy pits of darkness, where they are being held until the day of judgment" (2 Peter 2:4). Their fall was the result of seeking power and authority that God did not give them: "I remind you of the angels who did not stay within the limits of authority God gave them but left the place where they belonged. God has kept them securely chained in prisons of darkness, waiting for the great day of judgment" (Jude 1:6).

This vivid description of the demons' captivity is likely *proleptic*, meaning it describes their future state as a present event. The Bible clearly indicates that demons are active in the world today.

So, what do demons do? They can possess people and cause both physical and spiritual harm. The story of the man with many demons ("Legion") in Mark 5:1-20 is a case in point. Throughout Scripture, demons seek to inflict harm and lead people astray.

Satan and his demons, above all, seek to keep people from hearing the good news of Jesus Christ: "Satan, who is the god of this world, has blinded the minds of those who don't believe. They are unable to see the glorious light of the Good News. They don't understand this message about the glory of Christ, who is the exact likeness of God" (2 Corinthians 4:4).

Demons are continuously deceiving people (2 Corinthians 11:14). They attempt to make evil look good and to entice even God's people to do evil.

One of the greatest dangers to God's churches and to

God's people is the teaching of false doctrine. Satan and his demons thus seek to lead us away from the truths of Scripture and to turn to false beliefs that will harm us, the church, and the world. "The Holy Spirit tells us clearly," Paul writes, "that in the last times some will turn away from the true faith; they will follow deceptive spirits and teachings that come from demons" (1 Timothy 4:1).

Satan and his demons will oppose Christians and torment them repeatedly. Paul, when speaking about his thorn in the flesh, described it as "a messenger from Satan to torment me and keep me from becoming proud" (2 Corinthians 12:7).

While demons are clearly powerful, they are limited by God. They certainly do not have the power of God. They are not omnipotent (all powerful), omniscient (all knowing), or omnipresent (the ability to be everywhere at once). We can and should defeat the demons. We are given the full armor of God to resist them and have victory on every front (Ephesians 6:10-17). When you clothe yourself in the armor, "you will be able to resist the enemy in the time of evil. Then after the battle you will still be standing firm" (Ephesians 6:13).

SATAN

Satan is the leader of the demons. The description of the work of demons is also ascribed to him. The names used to identify Satan in the Bible are telling. He is "the evil one" (Matthew 13:19); "the commander of the powers in the unseen world" (Ephesians 2:2); "the prince of demons" (Matthew 10:25); and, of course, "the devil" (Matthew 4:1).

Perhaps the name given to him that best describes his activity is "the enemy" (Luke 10:19). Satan is the enemy of God and opposes the will of God. As a consequence, he is our enemy as well. Believers have been given the Great Commission to take the gospel to the world and make disciples. As we obey this command, Satan will oppose us at every turn.

But, as noted above regarding demons, we do not have to succumb to Satan's wiles. In Luke 10:19, Jesus says, "Look, I have given you authority over all the power of the enemy." This statement is comprehensive. We can have authority over *all* the power of Satan.

Such is the reason we must put on the full armor of God, as noted earlier. Putting on the full armor includes spending time in the Bible ("Take the sword of the Spirit, which is the word of God" [Ephesians 6:17]) and prayer. Indeed, Paul concludes his description of the full armor with a plea for prayer: "Pray in the Spirit at all times and on every occasion. Stay alert and be persistent in your prayers for all believers everywhere" (Ephesians 6:18).

Angels are real; fallen angels, called demons, are real; and the chief demon, called Satan, is real. But the Bible teaches us that believers have no need to fear demons, nor should we have a defeatist attitude about them. We would not be told to stand firm against the devil if we could not resist him (1 Peter 5:9).

We believers have the Holy Spirit living in us. He is all we need to resist and defeat the enemy. As the apostle John reminds us, "You belong to God, my dear children. You have already won a victory over those people, because the Spirit who lives in you is greater than the spirit who lives in the world" (1 John 4:4).

As believers, we have all we need to fight the battles that come our way, and it has already been determined that Christ will win the war: "Then I saw an angel coming down from heaven with the key to the bottomless pit and a heavy chain in his hand. He seized the dragon—that old serpent, who is the devil, Satan—and bound him in chains for a thousand years" (Revelation 20:1-2).

There are different views on the thousand years, what we call the Millennium. Thus, the idea of Satan being bound for a thousand years is somewhat different from each perspective. However, we can be assured that, in every view, the defeat of Satan will one day be permanent.

The book of Revelation clearly notes the defeat of Satan and his demons, and it also demonstrates the joy of victory that is Christ's. Millions of angels worship together and acclaim, "Worthy is the Lamb who was slaughtered—to receive power and riches and wisdom and strength and honor and glory and blessing. . . . Blessing and glory and wisdom and thanksgiving and honor and power and strength belong to our God forever and ever!" (Revelation 5:12; 7:12).

Christ is triumphant. And we, in his power, are triumphant as well.

"I am convinced that nothing can ever separate us from God's love. Neither death nor life, neither angels nor demons, neither our fears for today nor our worries about tomorrow—not even the powers of hell can separate us from God's love" (Romans 8:38).

DISCUSSION QUESTIONS

1. Why is it critically important to recognize the unseen reality of angels and demons?

2. Name some of the actions of demons in the world today. How could they affect you?

3. What are some positive actions we can take as believers to win the battles of spiritual warfare?

8

I BELIEVE JESUS DIED FOR OUR SINS

Several years ago, I was in a deep conversation with a physician who was a member of the church where I served as pastor. Jim had spent several months examining the physical and medical issues related to the Crucifixion. He knew he was not the first person to do this research, but he wanted to see the facts for himself.

He invited me to lunch to share some of his findings. I fully expected him to give me a detailed explanation of the physical agony of the cross. Because Jim was a brilliant physician, I also expected to hear some of the medical details about crucifixion, particularly Jesus' crucifixion. Though my expectations were met, I was also surprised by the direction our conversation went.

Though I cannot recall the exact words he used, I remember Jim putting down his fork midway through our meal and speaking with obvious emotion.

"Thom, I started this journey expecting to get all the scientific and medical details of the crucifixion of Jesus," he began. "But this work did something to me I did not expect."

I waited while Jim regathered his composure.

"In my examination of the Cross," he resumed, "I certainly verified the agony Jesus suffered. And I certainly have a better perspective of the medical issues of his death. But the more work I did from an empirical and medical view, the more I realized what Jesus did for me. It's not just that it was an agonizing death, Thom. It wasn't just his suffering. It was that he died for *me*. He took capital punishment for *me*. He took what *I* deserved so I could be forgiven and have eternal life."

Admittedly, I was moved by Jim's emotions. I saw how much he had absorbed of what Jesus had done for him. Perhaps I needed to do some of my own prayerful study of the Cross. Perhaps I wasn't fully grasping the power of Jesus' crucifixion.

THE MAIN ISSUE

What is the most popular verse in the Bible? You probably know the answer. Most studies confirm that John 3:16 is still the most read and most popular verse.[3] In a conversation with Nicodemus, Jesus said, "This is how God loved the world: He gave his one and only Son, so that everyone who believes in him will not perish but have eternal life" (John 3:16).

The verse is incredibly rich and full of meaning. It begins with Jesus describing the primary way in which God has shown his love for us. The verse is powerfully clear that God *gave* his Son. He gave Jesus to us to live on earth and to die for our sins. The Son's life and death would become our gateway to eternal life. It is little wonder this verse is so popular.

The apostle Paul was unequivocal about the necessity of the Cross: "God presented Jesus as the sacrifice for sin. People are made right with God when they believe that Jesus sacrificed his life, shedding his blood" (Romans 3:25). Sin demands punishment: "The wages of sin is death" (Romans 6:23). Though we deserve death for our sins, God sent Jesus in our place. He made the sacrifice. He shed his blood.

This act of self-sacrifice is known as the Atonement. It means that the price of sin has been paid by Jesus. Look at the full text of Romans 6:23: "For the wages of sin is death, but the free gift of God is eternal life through Christ Jesus our Lord." God not only forgives us through a punishment Christ did not deserve, but he also gives us eternal life. We can stand in God's presence as sin-free. This is why Romans 3:25 says we are "made right with God."

THE NATURE OF CHRIST'S DEATH ON THE CROSS

Again, John 3:16 reminds us "that everyone who believes in [Jesus] will not perish but have eternal life." The moment we trust Christ and believe in his act of obedient sacrifice on the cross, our sins are forgiven. But we all will sin again after we trust in Christ. No one aside from Jesus himself will live a sinless, perfect life. Does this mean we have to trust in Christ again and again to make certain our sins are forgiven and "up to date"? Not at all.

Christ led a perfect life, a sin-free life. God now counts the merits of Jesus' obedience on our behalf. This means we have our sins forgiven—past and present. And any future sins will not be counted against us because we have Christ's righteousness upon us. Paul affirms that "Christ's one act of righteousness brings a right relationship with God and new life for everyone. Because one person disobeyed God, many became sinners. But because one other person obeyed God, many will be made righteous" (Romans 5:18-19).

As my physician friend noted, the nature of Christ's death on the cross was excruciating. Ultimately, death by crucifixion was death by suffocation. Because of how Jesus was nailed to the cross, he had to push up with his legs and pull up with his hands to get a breath. Of course, his hands and feet were the points where the large nails had been driven. Each attempt to breathe was excruciating as the nails touched his nerves in his arms and feet and sent searing pains throughout his body. At some point, Jesus was no longer able to push up for air. He suffocated and died.

While the physical agony of the Crucifixion was intense, the spiritual agony was greater. Christ took the punishment from God for the sins of the world. Peter notes, "He personally carried our sins in his body on the cross so that we can be dead to sin and live for what is right. By his wounds you are healed" (1 Peter 2:24). Jesus was totally forsaken on the cross. His closest followers had abandoned him. And as he took our sins upon himself, even his heavenly Father turned his back on him. Jesus cried out, "'*Eli, Eli, lema sabachthani?*' which means 'My God, my God, why have you abandoned me?'" (Matthew 27:46).

Christ's death on the cross is sometimes called substitutionary atonement, a big phrase that simply means Jesus took our place on the cross to pay for our sins. When Jesus rose from the dead, he asked, "Wasn't it clearly predicted that the Messiah would have to suffer all these things before entering his glory?" (Luke 24:26). Of course, Jesus' question was rhetorical. He was explaining clearly that his death on the cross was the plan of God.

THE OLD TESTAMENT FORESHADOWS
THE ULTIMATE SACRIFICE

The Old Testament continually and consistently points to Jesus. In fact, we can understand the Old Testament much more clearly if we see Jesus as the central theme.

The sacrificial system of animals in the Old Testament points to Christ. It was a powerful reminder of the seriousness of sin. Since "the wages of sin is death" (Romans 6:23), a life had to be sacrificed for sin. In the Old Testament system, an animal was used as a substitute for those who had sinned. The animal could have no defects; it had to be spotless. The person offering the sacrifice had to identify with the animal, often by putting his hand on it. And the one offering the sacrifice had to take the life of the animal and shed its blood.

Animal sacrifices were a clear foreshadowing of Christ's death on the cross. He was perfect and sinless, "without defects." Like the animal, he was the substitute for sinners. He identified with us, sinners in need of forgiveness. And his blood was shed; his life was taken. Hebrews 10:1 notes, "The old system under the law of Moses was only a shadow, a dim preview of the good things to come, not the good things themselves. The sacrifices under that system were repeated again and again, year after year, but they were never able to provide perfect cleansing for those who came to worship."

Comparing animal sacrifices to Jesus' own sacrifice, the writer of Hebrews says, "Just think how much more the blood of Christ will purify our consciences from sinful deeds so that we can worship the living God. For by the power of the eternal Spirit, Christ offered himself to God as a perfect sacrifice for our sins" (Hebrews 9:14).

The Old Testament system of repeated animal sacrifices is no longer necessary because Christ is our once-and-for-all-time sacrifice. Again, the writer of Hebrews sums it up powerfully:

> Just as each person is destined to die once and after that comes judgment, so also Christ was offered once for all time as a sacrifice to take away the sins of many people. He will come again, not to deal with our sins, but to bring salvation to all who are eagerly waiting for him.
> HEBREWS 9:27-28

John the Baptist "saw Jesus coming toward him and said, 'Look! The Lamb of God who takes away the sin of the world!'" (John 1:29). John recognized that Jesus was the final sacrifice; thus, he calls him "the Lamb." Christ is the fulfillment of the Old Testament sacrificial system and the final sacrifice that will ever need to be made.

THE RESULT OF JESUS' DEATH ON THE CROSS

The picture of Jesus' death on the cross came into clearer focus for my physician friend Jim. He began to see more poignantly the physical and spiritual agony Jesus suffered for him and for all who believe in Christ. The Cross became intensely personal because it was an intensely personal sacrifice.

The writer of Hebrews notes that "according to the law of Moses, nearly everything was purified with blood. For without the shedding of blood, there is no forgiveness" (Hebrews 9:22). But Jesus' blood was shed as the final sacrifice. Because of that blood, the ultimate sacrifice has been made, and we can have forgiveness.

Do you see, then, why Jesus' death on the cross is not only important, but vitally necessary? Because his blood was shed, we can have the assurance that those who believe in him can have their sins forgiven. And because our sins are forgiven, we can boldly come into the presence of God. Paul writes, "He has rescued us from the kingdom of darkness and transferred us into the Kingdom of his dear Son, who purchased our freedom and forgave our sins" (Colossians 1:13-14).

THE VICTORY

Earlier I wrote about my hair stylist, who is not a Christian. She struggles with the idea that she can be forgiven. It seems to be her number one stumbling block to accepting Jesus. Every time I get my hair cut, I share more with her about what Jesus did on the cross, and why he went to the cross. Gradually, the fog seems to be lifting.

Like everyone else—including you and me—she does not *deserve* to be saved; but by Christ's death on the cross, she *can* be saved. Her sins can be forgiven. She can receive the gift of eternal life.

The Cross is a picture of a gruesome death. But for those of us who believe in what was accomplished there, it can be a picture of joyous victory. "Sin is the sting that results in death, and the law gives sin its power. But thank God! He gives us victory over sin and death through our Lord Jesus Christ" (1 Corinthians 15:56-57).

DISCUSSION QUESTIONS

1. Why is John 3:16 such a popular verse? How does it relate to Jesus' death on the cross?

2. Explain in your own words the meaning of *substitutionary atonement*.

3. How did the Old Testament foreshadow Jesus' death on the cross?

9

I BELIEVE IN THE RESURRECTION AND THE ASCENSION

The resurrection of Jesus Christ is central to the Bible and our faith. As the apostle Paul said, "If Christ has not been raised, then your faith is useless and you are still guilty of your sins. In that case, all who have died believing in Christ are lost! And if our hope in Christ is only for this life, we are more to be pitied than anyone in the world" (1 Corinthians 15:17-19).

Without the Resurrection, our faith is useless. Without the Resurrection, our sins are not forgiven. Without the Resurrection, we are lost. Without the Resurrection, we will not be with Christ in heaven. Happily, Paul concluded that "in fact, Christ has been raised from the dead. He is the first of a great harvest of all who have died" (1 Corinthians 15:20).

THE CENTRALITY OF THE RESURRECTION

After Peter's salutation in his first letter, he points to the centrality of the Resurrection with the following declaration: "All praise to God, the Father of our Lord Jesus Christ. It is by his great mercy that we have been born again, because God raised Jesus Christ from the dead. Now we live with great expectation" (1 Peter 1:3).

In one verse, Peter ties the Resurrection to the mercy of God in our lives, to our salvation, and to the anticipation of seeing Christ again. By the time the first-century churches received this letter, it was commonly known that Jesus had died on a cross and then been raised from the dead three days later. The Resurrection was central to the first-century Christians and the churches they served.

Peter further reminds the church that the Resurrection is "a priceless inheritance—an inheritance that is kept in heaven for you, pure and undefiled, beyond the reach of change and decay. And through your faith, God is protecting you by his power until you receive this salvation, which is ready to be revealed on the last day for all to see" (1 Peter 1:4-5). The power of the Resurrection is immediate for everyone who has faith, and that power will keep us until we see Christ face-to-face. At that moment, our impure, defiled bodies will be given over to bodies that are pure and undefiled.

Simply stated, as believers we have the power of the

Resurrection to save us, keep us, and give us our perfect bodies in eternity. Our resurrected bodies will be much different from that of a person raised from the dead in his natural body, like Lazarus. Instead, we can look to the resurrected body of Jesus, which was perfect.

The disciples "ate and drank with him after he rose from the dead" (Acts 10:41). Luke says "he took the bread and blessed it. Then he broke it and gave it to them" (Luke 24:30). And Thomas asked to see the nail prints in Jesus' hands and the pierced point in his side. Jesus told him, "Put your finger here, and look at my hands. Put your hand into the wound in my side. Don't be faithless any longer. Believe!" (John 20:27). The Resurrection is a reality. Jesus affirmed beyond a doubt that his resurrected body was real when he said, "Look at my hands. Look at my feet. You can see that it's really me. Touch me and make sure that I am not a ghost, because ghosts don't have bodies, as you see that I do" (Luke 24:39).

The four Gospels all record the resurrection of Jesus. Again, the Resurrection is central to the Bible and our faith in general, and to each of the Gospel accounts specifically. While Matthew's Gospel briefly presents the resurrected Jesus, he focuses more attention on the empty tomb. When Mary Magdalene and "the other Mary" went to visit Jesus' tomb, they were surprised to see the rock rolled back from the mouth of the grave. But an angel told them, "Don't be afraid! . . . I know you are looking for Jesus, who was crucified. He isn't here! He is risen from the dead, just as he said would happen. Come, see where his body was lying" (Matthew 28:5-6).

Mark's account of the Resurrection is similar, but it adds that while on their way to the tomb the women discussed how they could roll away the rock since they wanted to anoint Jesus' body with burial spices. They asked, "Who will roll away the stone for us from the entrance to the tomb?" (Mark 16:3).

Luke has a much longer account of the Resurrection, a total of fifty-three verses (Luke 24:1-53). Luke is ever the historian with an eye for detail. He includes many of the words of the resurrected Jesus. For Luke, Christ's words bring added importance and validity to the Resurrection. Luke also ends his Gospel with the ascension of Jesus, which he repeats in Acts 1:9-11.

John's report of the Resurrection likewise includes significant details (John 20 and 21), especially about how the resurrected Jesus interacted with the women who followed him and with his disciples. It is Peter, however, who is the focus of John's attention. He includes the poignant conversation of Jesus asking Peter three times if the disciple really loved him.

None of the four Gospels would be complete without an account of the Resurrection. Though each Gospel writer has his own unique perspective, they all affirm the centrality of the Resurrection. Each writer also concludes his narrative with the Resurrection. That is to be expected from a chronological perspective, but it is more than that. The Resurrection is the pinnacle story of Christ's life on earth. His death and resurrection are indispensable truths to the Christian faith.

THE CONSEQUENCES OF THE RESURRECTION

The essential celebration of the Resurrection affirms that Jesus lives—and so can we. Jesus defeated death, and his victory is available to all who place their faith in him. Paul said that "God will raise us from the dead by his power, just as he raised our Lord from the dead" (1 Corinthians 6:14). The truth is powerfully clear: God's power raised his Son from the dead, and the same power can raise us from the dead.

Sin is death. The Resurrection conquers both sin and death. Paul reminds us with acclamation that

> When our dying bodies have been transformed into bodies that will never die, this Scripture will be fulfilled: "Death is swallowed up in victory. O death, where is your victory? O death, where is your sting?" For sin is the sting that results in death, and the law gives sin its power. But thank God! He gives us victory over sin and death through our Lord Jesus Christ.
> 1 CORINTHIANS 15:54-57

Paul teaches that the Resurrection defeated sin.

> Since we died with Christ, we know we will also live with him. We are sure of this because Christ was raised from the dead, and he will never die again. Death no longer has any power over him. When he died, he died once to break the power of sin. But now that he lives, he lives for the glory of God. So you also should consider yourselves to be dead to the power of sin and alive to God through Christ Jesus.
> ROMANS 6:8-11

The Resurrection defeated death for those who believe. The Resurrection defeated sin for those who believe.

Justification means to be made right with God. Because of sin, we were separated from God. Because of the Cross and the Resurrection, we are able to come before God fully justified. Paul made this point when he said, "We know that God, who raised the Lord Jesus, will also raise us with Jesus and present us to himself together with you" (2 Corinthians 4:14). When we are presented to God, we will have all the righteousness of Christ because of his death and resurrection.

The Resurrection means we are made right with God.

The Resurrection also means we will one day get new bodies. We caught a glimpse of what these bodies will be like by reading about Jesus' resurrected body. Paul said that "our earthly bodies are planted in the ground when we die, but they will be raised to live forever" (1 Corinthians 15:42). And our new bodies will never die nor grow old; "our mortal bodies must be transformed into immortal bodies" (1 Corinthians 15:53).

Is it any wonder the Resurrection is central to life today and life hereafter? When Jesus rose from the dead, he changed the course of the world forever. And for those who believe in him, the promises and hope are beyond measure.

I believe in the Resurrection.

I BELIEVE IN THE ASCENSION

Some scholars treat the Ascension as its own unique doctrine. Others see it as the continuation and culmination of the Resurrection. Mark, in his own unique and to-the-point style of writing, describes the Ascension with brevity: "When the Lord Jesus had finished talking with them, he was taken up into heaven and sat down in the place of honor at God's right hand" (Mark 16:19). For Mark, the Ascension ended Jesus' time on earth in his resurrected body. The Ascension completed the Resurrection. The Ascension means that Jesus physically departed from earth by rising into heaven. This event occurred on the fortieth day after the Resurrection.

Fortunately, Luke gives us a bit more detail about the

Ascension in his two books, Luke and Acts. His account in Luke is brief, much like Mark's account: "While he was blessing them, he left them and was taken up to heaven" (24:51). Like Mark, Luke sees the Ascension as the culmination of the Resurrection.

In the book of Acts, Luke gives us more details. First, he records Jesus telling his followers that the Holy Spirit would soon come upon them: "You will receive power when the Holy Spirit comes upon you" (Acts 1:8). He next leaves them the command to fulfill the Great Commission: "You will be my witnesses, telling people about me everywhere—in Jerusalem, throughout Judea, in Samaria, and to the ends of the earth" (Acts 1:8).

Luke uses the monumental occasion of the Ascension to prepare Christ's followers for the coming of the Holy Spirit. Christ had promised his Spirit would come to teach them once he left. Jesus said, "It is best for you that I go away, because if I don't, the Advocate won't come. If I do go away, then I will send him to you" (John 16:7).

The Ascension was also the moment for Jesus to let his followers know that they would be completing his mission on earth. They would be sharing the good news of the gospel all over the world. And lest they think they were not prepared or able to carry out the mission, he reminded them that the Holy Spirit would always be with them.

Luke also uses the seconds after the Ascension to draw a

somewhat humorous picture of the followers of Christ staring into the empty space above where Christ had just been taken up. Two angels ("two white-robed men" [Acts 1:10]) tell them they can stop staring because "someday [Jesus] will return from heaven in the same way you saw him go!" (Acts 1:11).

In many ways, the Ascension is indeed an extension of the Resurrection story. In other ways, it is its own unique doctrine and has its own place in the Bible. But through Luke's eyewitness account recorded in Acts 1:11, we see the Ascension as a precursor to the return of Christ. He will indeed return someday in the same way he left. We wait eagerly with all creation "for that future day" (Romans 8:19).

"Look! He comes with the clouds of heaven. And everyone will see him—even those who pierced him. And all the nations of the world will mourn for him. Yes! Amen!" (Revelation 1:7).

DISCUSSION QUESTIONS

1. How was Jesus' resurrected body like our bodies today? How was his body different from our bodies today?

2. What are the differences in the perspectives of the Resurrection in the four Gospels: Matthew, Mark, Luke, and John?

3. How might the Ascension be seen as the culmination of the Resurrection?

10

I BELIEVE CHRIST IS THE ONLY WAY OF SALVATION

Shortly before I wrote this book, I had a conversation with a man who has done some work for me over the years. Andre started the conversation talking about politics, but I gently moved the discussion to another topic. It wasn't unusual for the two of us to have discussions that some might consider a bit sensitive. Though we don't know each other well, we've spoken often enough to be comfortable in our conversations.

In my more recent conversations with Andre, I had begun moving the topic to matters of faith. Though he responded politely, he never really let me move the conversation forward. This time, however, he didn't stop me when I started talking about my beliefs.

Andre knows I'm a Christian, but it became obvious in

the course of our conversation that he wasn't fully informed on what it means to be a Christian. He views himself as open-minded, and he made a comment I've heard countless times: "It's fine for you to believe in Jesus, Thom, just like it's fine for other people to believe in their idea of who God is."

There is a major problem with Andre's statement. If we're concerned about their salvation, it is *not* fine for people to believe that there are ways to God apart from Jesus. The main objection comes from Jesus himself, who said, "I am the way, the truth, and the life. No one can come to the Father except through me" (John 14:6). Jesus could not have said it more clearly. If you believe in any way other than Jesus, you will not get to God. You will not get to heaven.

There are five ways we can look at how people believe in God. Let's view them from the broadest to the narrowest.

Atheism is the belief that there is no God. Closely related to atheism is *agnosticism*, a belief that expresses uncertainty about God's existence. The word literally means "don't know." Agnostics don't know, but atheists say with certainty there is no God. Either way, God's presence, and the path to him, is not affirmed.

Universalism affirms the presence of God and believes that everyone will get to him, one way or another. It is sometimes expressed as "God will save everyone."

When you believe there are multiple paths to God, you

hold to the belief of *pluralism*. Whereas universalism says you don't have to believe in anything or anyone to get to heaven, pluralism says you have to believe in something. If you are a Muslim, Christian, Hindu, or some other form of religion, pluralism says you are on the right path to God.

Inclusivism is a nuanced belief. It affirms that Christ is the only way of salvation but says that people can come to Christ "anonymously." For example, if you believe that Hinduism is a path to God, Jesus will appropriate that belief as trusting in him. Inclusivism is really a form of pluralism with Jesus thrown in the mix in name only.

Jesus and the Bible teach *exclusivism*. Jesus is the only way of salvation, and one must have explicit faith in him. Exclusivism is taught by Christ in John 14:6. It is the narrowest of all the paths to God, which is exactly what Jesus taught. He said, "You can enter God's Kingdom only through the narrow gate. The highway to hell is broad, and its gate is wide for the many who choose that way. But the gateway to life is very narrow and the road is difficult, and only a few ever find it" (Matthew 7:13-14).

THE RESISTED DOCTRINE

The doctrine of exclusivity, the belief that Jesus is the only way of salvation, has been resisted throughout history. The

Pharisees attempted to kill Jesus after he claimed to be God when "they picked up stones to throw at him" (John 8:59). They did not want to hear that Jesus is the path to God. It didn't fit their beliefs, and it threatened their power.

Today, the doctrine of exclusivity is often perceived as narrow-minded and prejudicial. The critics assume that it is some type of exclusive society that seeks to exclude others. But the narrow way is not the result of Jesus excluding people; it is the decision of those who are excluded. John 3:16 clearly states that "everyone who believes in him [Jesus] will not perish but have eternal life." The offer is for everyone to gain eternal life. It is not a narrow-minded belief, but it *is* a narrow way.

Jesus affirmed that he would respond to those who seek him: "Keep on asking, and you will receive what you ask for. Keep on seeking, and you will find. Keep on knocking, and the door will be opened to you. For everyone who asks, receives. Everyone who seeks, finds. And to everyone who knocks, the door will be opened" (Matthew 7:7-8). God offers salvation to all who ask for it, but it must be on his terms, not based on some human-centered concept.

Ultimately, the exclusive gospel is broad in its invitation but narrow in its application. Anyone by faith can receive Christ. But Christ is not just *a way* to God; he is *the way* to God.

WHY IS CHRIST THE ONLY WAY?

Simply stated, Christ is God. Because he is God, he is likewise the only path to God. There are at least five reasons to affirm Christ as the only way of salvation.

First, Christ alone was conceived by the Holy Spirit and born of a virgin. His conception and birth were both miraculous. No one has ever come into the world as Jesus did. Of course, he came as a man so he could live a perfect life and become the perfect sacrifice for our sins.

Second, Christ alone is both fully human and fully God. As we discussed in chapter 3, that's a difficult concept to grasp. But Jesus is our living example. Only he is both man and God.

Third, Christ lived a sinless life. He faced temptation, but he did not yield to temptation. John reminds us that "Jesus came to take away our sins, and there is no sin in him" (1 John 3:5). No one apart from Jesus has ever lived a life of perfection. Thus, only Jesus is qualified to be our Savior.

Fourth, Jesus died on the cross as our substitute. His death was the only acceptable way for God to forgive our sins. No one else in history has ever made such a sacrifice because no one in history has ever been qualified. The perfect man became the perfect substitute to receive God's punishment. Because God is perfect holiness, he could not look at sin without compromising that holiness. So he sent Jesus to do for us what we could never do for ourselves. Jesus took away our sin so that God looks upon Christians as people with sinless holiness.

Fifth, Jesus rose from the dead and ascended to heaven. Only God has the power to defeat death, and he accomplished it by raising Jesus from the dead. As a person of the Trinity, Jesus was truly God being raised from the dead and soon ascending to heaven.

The conclusion is simple but powerful. Jesus demonstrated clearly that he is God. Not only is he God, but he is the only path of salvation to God. No one, no other god, no other belief system can claim or do what Jesus did.

THE IMPLICATIONS OF SALVATION THROUGH CHRIST ALONE

One of the most significant implications of the doctrine of exclusivity is the affirmation of God's love for us. Isn't that the essence of John 3:16? God loves us so much that he provided the way of salvation, a way that would not have been available by any other means. We did not deserve to be saved, but God provided a way because of his love for us.

Related to God's love is the love of Christ demonstrated by his willingness to be our Savior. His sacrifice was immense. His pain was beyond our comprehension. Shortly before he was arrested, Jesus told his disciples, "My soul is crushed with grief to the point of death" (Matthew 26:38). Then, when Jesus prayed to God the Father, he said, "My Father! If it is possible, let this cup of suffering be taken away from me. Yet I want your will to be done, not mine" (Matthew 26:39).

Christ anticipated the agony of the Cross. He knew the pain he was about to face. Yet he was willing to move forward for two key reasons. First, he was always obedient to the Father, who sent him on this mission. Second, he knew his death and resurrection would be the only way of salvation for humanity. All of humanity would be doomed outside of his obedience.

We also see the foundations of the Great Commission implicit in the doctrine of exclusivity. Since Christ is the only way of salvation, it is imperative that we tell others this message. We call it "sharing the gospel" or "sharing the Good News." It is instructive to see what Jesus' last words were to his followers before he ascended to heaven: "I have been given all authority in heaven and on earth. Therefore, go and make disciples of all the nations, baptizing them in the name of the Father and the Son and the Holy Spirit" (Matthew 28:18-19).

Luke records a similar command in Acts 1:8: "You will receive power when the Holy Spirit comes upon you. And you will be my witnesses, telling people about me everywhere— in Jerusalem, throughout Judea, in Samaria, and to the ends of the earth."

These two Great Commission passages have three things in common. First, they were both recorded shortly before Jesus ascended to heaven. In that light, they are a last will and testament to his followers, a command of the utmost importance. Second, they clearly say that we will have Christ's power to share the gospel. Matthew points to Christ's authority, and Luke refers to the power of the Holy Spirit.

Third, both passages are mandates to Christ's followers to *go* and *tell*. His death and resurrection were for a reason. Since he is the only way of salvation, we must share that message at every opportunity. We must have the boldness of Peter and John. The two disciples were arrested for telling people about Jesus. When they were brought before the members of the council, they were told to stop speaking in the name of Jesus.

If Peter and John would have immediately obeyed those orders, they would have been released unharmed. Instead, they said, "We cannot stop telling about everything we have seen and heard" (Acts 4:20). And just moments before they made that statement, they had boldly declared the exclusivity of salvation through Christ: "There is salvation in no one else! God has given no other name under heaven by which we must be saved" (Acts 4:12).

Thus, the exclusivity of salvation through Christ for these two disciples was inextricably tied to sharing the gospel.

Since Jesus is the only way, we must tell others this good news with urgency.

Throughout the New Testament, there is an underlying message that cannot be avoided: Followers of Jesus paid a price for sharing the Good News. For example, just after Jesus had ascended, as the early church was getting on its feet, Peter and John faced beatings and imprisonment for their faithful testimony.

Sometimes, the early witnesses paid with their lives, as Stephen did in Acts 7.

Why should we, then, not expect to pay a price for faithfully sharing the gospel of Christ in our day? The world has never welcomed the doctrine of the exclusivity of Christ. In fact, at many points in history, the world has responded violently to those who share the gospel. Even today, Christians are martyred with shocking and regular violence.

It is likely you will find yourself in a culture that rejects the truth that Christ is the only way of salvation. You might be ostracized. You might anger friends. You might lose your job. And in some places in the world today, you might die.

But the most unloving thing we can do is remain silent. How can we be reluctant to share the best news there ever was? How can we be hesitant to let people know that Christ is the only way of salvation?

It is both our privilege and our command. We know the truth. Christ is the only way of salvation. Now we must tell that truth to others. Like Peter and John, "we cannot stop telling about everything we have seen and heard" (Acts 4:20).

DISCUSSION QUESTIONS

1. What are the differences between *atheism, universalism, pluralism, inclusivism*, and *exclusivism*?

2. What do we mean when we say that the exclusive gospel is broad in its invitation but narrow in its application?

3. How should the belief that Christ is the only way of salvation affect our personal evangelism; that is, our attitudes and actions about sharing the gospel?

11

I BELIEVE IN
THE LOCAL CHURCH

The church is one of the most dominant themes and emphases in the New Testament. Sadly, it is also taken for granted by many Christians in numerous parts of the world today. We must see the big picture. We must see the importance of the church in the Bible.

The church was important to Jesus. When he asked his disciples who they thought he was, Peter said, "You are the Messiah, the Son of the living God." Peter got it right, so Jesus responded by saying, "You are blessed, Simon son of John, because my Father in heaven has revealed this to you. You did not learn this from any human being. Now I say to you that you are Peter (which means 'rock'), and upon this rock I will build my church, and all the powers of hell will not conquer it" (Matthew 16:16-18).

When Peter confessed Jesus as the Messiah, the moment became foundational for building the church. Jesus knew that his mission after his death and resurrection would be in the hands of men and women in churches around the world. The church was his plan A. He did not give us a plan B. Though Jesus taught his disciples directly, he left us the Holy Spirit to carry out that mission in our churches (John 14:16).

The New Testament as a whole and in each of its books affirms the importance of the church. The first church began in Jerusalem right after Jesus ascended to heaven. Luke captured some of the details of those formative moments: "Those who believed what Peter said were baptized and added to the church that day—about 3,000 in all. All the believers devoted themselves to the apostles' teaching, and to fellowship, and to sharing in meals (including the Lord's Supper), and to prayer" (Acts 2:41-42).

So, immediately after Jesus ascended and Peter preached his sermon in Jerusalem, a church was born. The book of Acts provides a historical glimpse of the beginning of churches in the Roman Empire and beyond. The rest of the New Testament is largely centered around local churches in different locations, in the form of letters to those churches or to leaders in those churches. Additionally, the first three chapters of the book of Revelation are messages to and about seven local churches.

We cannot overlook the importance of the church in the Bible. The church was important to Jesus, and the church is the key focal point of the New Testament from Acts to Revelation.

THE LOCAL CHURCH AND THE UNIVERSAL CHURCH

Sometimes a distinction is made between the local church and all believers in Christ—that is, the universal church, or invisible church. The local church, of course, consists of believers gathering and ministering in a specific place. The term *universal* is an all-inclusive term meant to encompass every believer around the globe. *Invisible* means that these believers are not at a specific address; or, in some cases, it means that only God can know for certain the hearts of those who have placed their faith in Jesus Christ.

It is not unusual to see writers capitalize *Church* when referring to the universal church and to use a lowercase *c* when referring to a local gathering of believers. Most Bible translations lowercase *church* in both instances. For example, Paul, in writing about the universal church, says that "God has put all things under the authority of Christ and has made him head over all things for the benefit of the *church*" (Ephesians 1:22, italics added). More often, Paul wrote about the local church, as in this salutation to the church of Philippi: "This letter is from Paul and Timothy, slaves of Christ Jesus. I am writing to all of God's holy people in Philippi who belong to Christ Jesus, including the *church* leaders and deacons" (Philippians 1:1, italics added).

Both the universal church and the local church are important. But after the four Gospels, most of the New Testament is about matters in local churches.

WHY THE LOCAL CHURCH IS IMPORTANT FOR CHRISTIANS

Many of the conversations I've had with inactive church members have similar themes. First, I let them know we have missed them at church. Then they typically respond with something like this: "Jesus and I get along just fine by ourselves." The problem is that Jesus never intended for Christianity to be a solo act. The entirety of the New Testament is about believers on a mission together, not alone. The writer of Hebrews says it succinctly and specifically: "Let us not neglect our meeting together, as some people do, but encourage one another, especially now that the day of his return is drawing near" (Hebrews 10:25).

Another common comment about the local church goes something like this: "The church is the people, not the building." Yes, that statement is biblically correct, but it is typically misused. The person who makes the statement typically means that gathering in the building is not that important. Gathering is not only important; it is biblically imperative. We usually gather in a building, but, regardless, we are commanded to gather somewhere.

Yet a similar refrain today is, "It doesn't matter how many people attend; it matters how many people you send." Those two points are complementary, not mutually exclusive. We are supposed to be a church that attends *and* sends.

The New Testament assumes a common theme about the local church. It assumes Christians are connected to one another. It assumes Christians gather regularly in worship. It assumes that Christians are serving together in a local church. And it assumes Christians are members of a local church.

As Christians, we are called to serve. Paul clearly establishes that part of a church leader's responsibility is to "equip God's people to do his work and build up the church, the body of Christ" (Ephesians 4:12). Believers are to be prepared and enabled for service. Likewise, we are called to gather in worship as Christians. Both worship and service are presumed in Scripture in the context of living in community. When Paul wrote the letter to the church at Ephesus, a specific local church, he was likely envisioning this ministry taking place as the Ephesians served together. In his closing words, Paul reminds the church members to love one another as they work together serving and worshiping: "Be kind to each other, tenderhearted, forgiving one another, just as God through Christ has forgiven you" (Ephesians 4:32).

DOES MEMBERSHIP IN A LOCAL CHURCH MATTER?

Does it really matter whether we are members of a local church? Even more important, is church membership in the Bible? The answer to both questions is an emphatic *yes*.

Let's first deal with the word *member*. In Western culture, we often must first define what a "member" is not. The word is frequently used to describe one's affiliation with a country club or a civic club, as in "I am a member of the Rotary."

A country club member pays his or her dues and receives perks and benefits in return. Those benefits may include golf, swimming, meals, tennis, and many more. The basic idea is that you pay with the expectation of receiving something of value.

Civic club membership may have a more altruistic bent— that is, you pay your dues and also perform some service for the greater good of the community. But you still receive benefits, such as meals, entertainment, and activities for the money you pay.

If we take either of these concepts of membership— especially country club membership—into the local church, we will have problems.

The apostle Paul used the word *member* in an entirely

different context, drawing upon the metaphor of the human body to illustrate how each member is important.

> The body has many different parts, not just one part. If the foot says, "I am not a part of the body because I am not a hand," that does not make it any less a part of the body. And if the ear says, "I am not part of the body because I am not an eye," would that make it any less a part of the body? If the whole body were an eye, how would you hear? Or if your whole body were an ear, how would you smell anything?
> CORINTHIANS 12:14-17

Paul's point is that every part, or member, of the human body plays a vital role. Likewise, every member of the church, the body of Christ, plays a vital role, as each member performs his or her function and also cares for the other members: "This makes for harmony among the members, so that all the members care for each other" (1 Corinthians 12:25).

Church membership, then, is vastly different from civic club or country club membership. Church membership means we are to function actively in the congregation. It means we care for others. It means we give generously with no strings attached. Church membership means we serve instead of seeking to be served. It means we put ourselves last, just as Jesus told us (Matthew 20:16).

The New Testament never portrays a believer independent of a local church. Church membership is important because it is important in the Bible. Church membership is important because it's how we learn to serve, to give, to love, and to be held accountable.

Church membership is indeed important. I believe in the local church.

BIBLICAL METAPHORS OF THE CHURCH

The writers of Scripture use different metaphors to describe the church. As mentioned, Paul uses the entirety of 1 Corinthians 12 to illustrate the church as a body. Paul also compares the church to a family, in that both family members and church members relate to one another out of love and submission. Also using a familial metaphor, Paul presents Christ as the groom and the church as his bride (Ephesians 5:31-32).

There are other metaphors for the church as well. The church is a holy priesthood (1 Peter 2:4-9). The church is an olive tree with living branches (Romans 11:17-24). The church is a field with crops (1 Corinthians 3:5-9). The church is a building, with Christ as the foundation and others building upon it (1 Corinthians 3:9-15). Though the metaphors vary, they have common themes. Each suggests that members are part of a greater whole. Each metaphor is clear that, without the different parts, the whole would not exist. And the metaphors remind us that members are supposed to function for the greater good of the whole.

WHAT, THEN, IS A CHURCH?

If you are meeting with other people for prayer and Bible study, is your group a church? Probably not. The New Testament demonstrates gatherings to be churches when they carry out certain functions. Sometimes, these functions are called *marks*.

The polity and doctrine of a local church determines the marks of a particular congregation. For certain, most churches consider faithful biblical preaching to be a mark of a church. Paul instructed his protégé Timothy to "preach the word of God. Be prepared, whether the time is favorable or not. Patiently correct, rebuke, and encourage your people with good teaching" (2 Timothy 4:2).

A church also observes the Lord's Supper or Communion. Some churches call it an ordinance or a sacrament, but its purpose is to be a constant reminder of what Christ did for us through his death on the cross. Paul wrote in detail how a church should take the Lord's Supper, and he reminded us that "every time you eat this bread and drink this cup, you are announcing the Lord's death until he comes again" (1 Corinthians 11:26).

Whereas the Lord's Supper reminds us to remain in faithful fellowship in the church, baptism as an ordinance is an entry mark into the church. Jesus reminded the churches that would be established after his ascension of the importance of baptism in the name of the Trinity. We are to baptize "in the name of the Father and the Son and the Holy Spirit" (Matthew 28:19).

Church discipline is important in the New Testament, so some congregations add it as a mark of their local church. Paul was emphatic that an unrepentant and flagrant sinner could not continue fellowship in the church, so he told the leaders of the church that they "must remove the evil person from among you" (1 Corinthians 5:13). But Paul also spoke boldly about restoring a repentant believer: "Now, however, it is time to forgive and comfort him. Otherwise he may be overcome by discouragement. So I urge you now to reaffirm your love for him" (2 Corinthians 2:7-8). Church discipline has *correction* as its method and *restoration* as its goal.

I AM A CHURCH MEMBER

We received by faith the gift of salvation. It was totally undeserved, a gift of grace. That gift not only saved us, but it also made us a part of a family, a family we call the church. The church, then, is part of God's gift to us. Membership in the body of Christ is a gift from God, one we should not take lightly.

It is not a legalistic obligation. It doesn't come with country club perks. It's not a license for entitlements. It is a gift from God, a gift we should treasure. It is a gift we should receive with great joy and anticipation.

I am a church member.

Those five words describe the gift that has been given to believers. So, we respond to the gift with gratitude. We respond by serving others as Jesus served us. Churches would be a lot healthier if members decided to serve and put themselves last.

I believe in the church. And churches are healthy when their members serve sacrificially.

It can start with you.

DISCUSSION QUESTIONS

1. Explain how believers are part of both the universal church and the local church.

2. Why is it important for you to be committed, involved, and sacrificial in a local church?

3. Why is the human body a good metaphor for the church?

12

I BELIEVE CHRISTIANS ARE TO GROW SPIRITUALLY

When we become followers of Christ, we experience *regeneration*—which means we are born again or born a second time. This act of God takes place upon our repentance and placing faith in Christ. We were first born physically, and now we are born spiritually—our second birth. Regeneration also brings to us *justification*. To be justified is to be made right, and we are made right before God because of Jesus' work.

God justifies us when we repent and place our faith in Christ. But God also begins the process of *sanctification*, a word that means to be made holy or to be set apart. Perhaps the clearest way to grasp sanctification is that we are to become more like Jesus. He is perfect holiness. And though we will not be made perfect this side of heaven, we are to strive, in God's power, to be more like Christ.

Ideally, the process of sanctification begins in earnest when someone becomes a Christian. My own testimony, though, is one of a person for whom sanctification moved imperceptibly slowly.

I've shared the story of my salvation in several of my books. I was raised in a small town where I don't recall hearing the gospel preached in church. To be fair, the problem may have been my dull ears rather than unfaithful preaching. Still, I don't ever remember anyone in the pulpit or otherwise sharing with me the gospel message.

God blessed me with a godly high school coach by the name of Joe Hendrickson. Though I don't recall the specifics of what led to that particular moment, I remember Coach Joe telling me how I could become a Christian. I heard and understood the words *repent* and *faith* for the first time. Later in the day after he shared the gospel with me, I repented of my sins and placed my faith in Christ.

I remember feeling a deep hunger to learn more about this new faith God had given me, but I struggled through Genesis, Exodus, and Leviticus in the King James Version Bible that had been given to me when I was born.

I returned to church with a new zeal to be a follower of Christ, but when I found little encouragement and no direction for how I could grow spiritually as a believer, I began to revert to my old lifestyle. My sanctification, a word unknown to me at the time, seemed to come to a screeching halt.

But there was something different. When I rebelled and turned back to my life of sin, I felt conviction, or guilt. Even more, I knew I wanted something different. I knew that the life I was living was not the life I was supposed to be living.

Eventually, I met a teenage girl who gradually led me back to growth as a Christian. When we married a few years later, she asked if I would consider joining a church in our new town. Though I waited a couple of years before deciding, I became motivated to find a church when my wife said two key words to me: "I'm pregnant." That was the impetus I needed to get serious about finding a church. I wanted to be a godly dad and husband for my family.

Thankfully, the church we chose had solid biblical preaching and I was given a path to grow spiritually. This time around, I could sense I was growing in Christ every day. At age twenty-four, sanctification became real and evident in my life.

BABY CHRISTIANS AND MATURE CHRISTIANS

The apostle Paul was a master of metaphors, and he used the image of infants in Christ to describe those who were not growing spiritually. When he wrote the troubled church at Corinth, he said, "When I was with you I couldn't talk to you as I would to spiritual people. I had to talk as though you belonged to this world or as though you were infants in Christ. I had to feed you with milk, not with solid food, because you weren't ready for anything stronger" (1 Corinthians 3:1-2).

Looking back at my first few years as a Christian, I know now that I was a spiritual infant, a baby Christian. It was God's desire for me to grow spiritually. Even as a mature man today, I know I have a lot of growing to do. In God's power, I will strive to grow spiritually every day until I see him face-to-face.

SANCTIFICATION IS A PROCESS

It is evident, then, that sanctification is a process. As long as we are on this side of heaven, we will not be free from sin. John writes, "If we claim we have no sin, we are only fooling ourselves and not living in the truth" (1 John 1:8). John also reminds us that we should return to the path of sanctification by confessing our sins: "If we confess our sins to him, he is faithful and just to forgive us our sins and to cleanse us from all wickedness" (1 John 1:9).

Once we become followers of Christ, we have his power in us. We do not have to be controlled by sin. Paul writes, "Do not let sin control the way you live; do not give in to sinful desires" (Romans 6:12). Paul further exhorts us to "give yourselves completely to God, for you were dead, but now you have new life" (Romans 6:13). Before we became Christians, we were slaves to sin, but "sin is no longer your master, for you no longer live under the requirements of the law. Instead, you live under the freedom of God's grace" (Romans 6:14).

We will continue to grow spiritually, or grow in sanctification, until the Lord returns. Paul writes, "We are citizens of heaven, where the Lord Jesus Christ lives. And we are eagerly waiting for him to return as our Savior. He will take our weak mortal bodies and change them into glorious bodies like his own, using the same power with which he will bring everything under his control" (Philippians 3:20-21).

GOD'S POWER IN OUR SPIRITUAL GROWTH

We must begin with the clear understanding that spiritual growth comes from God. We can do nothing apart from his power. Paul wrote to the church at Thessalonica, "Now may the God of peace make you holy in every way, and may your whole spirit and soul and body be kept blameless until our Lord Jesus Christ comes again. God will make this happen, for he who calls you is faithful" (1 Thessalonians 5:23-24).

This passage powerfully depicts the work of God in our spiritual growth. First, it says that God is responsible for making us holy. Paul uses "make you holy" in the same sense we might use "grow spiritually." Next, he notes that our goal is to move toward becoming blameless. As we noted earlier, we do not attain perfection or blamelessness in this life, but we do strive toward it in God's power. Paul then mentions we will move in this path of sanctification until Christ returns. At that point, we will be given our resurrected bodies, which will be free from sin.

There is a strong word of assurance in 1 Thessalonians 5:24. Paul says, "God will make this happen." There is no room for doubt. His power is at work. Paul further reminds us that God is faithful. He has promised us his power and the presence of the Holy Spirit, and he will keep that promise.

Jesus promised us he would leave the Holy Spirit for us once he returned to heaven: "If you love me, obey my commandments. And I will ask the Father, and he will give you another Advocate, who will never leave you" (John 14:15-16). Jesus first commands us to obey his commandments. Such is the way we will grow in Christ. But he makes it clear that the Advocate, or the Holy Spirit, will empower us on this path of spiritual growth.

Peter writes in his letter to believers that "God the Father knew you and chose you long ago, and his Spirit has made you holy. As a result, you have obeyed him and have been cleansed by the blood of Jesus Christ" (1 Peter 1:2). Again, it is the Holy Spirit who makes us holy. It is the Holy Spirit who gives us the power to be obedient and, thus, to grow in our Christian faith.

That's why Paul said our spiritual growth is dependent on the Holy Spirit. We walk by the Spirit. We are filled with the Spirit. And when we grow as Christians, we bear the fruit of the Spirit. Paul notes that "the Holy Spirit produces this kind of fruit in our lives: love, joy, peace, patience, kindness, goodness, faithfulness, gentleness, and self-control" (Galatians 5:22-23).

OUR ROLE IN GROWING SPIRITUALLY

Paul addresses the tension between God's work and our role in growing spiritually when he says, "You have no obligation to do what your sinful nature urges you to do. For if you live by its dictates, you will die. But if through the power of the Spirit you put to death the deeds of your sinful nature, you will live" (Romans 8:12-13). On the one hand, Paul emphasizes that we are to live "through the power of the Spirit." On the other hand, there is a clear sense of the volitional nature of growing spiritually. We choose to grow closer to Christ, and we are empowered by the Spirit to do so.

Paul again reflects similar sentiments when he says, "Work hard to show the results of your salvation, obeying God with deep reverence and fear. For God is working in you, giving you the desire and the power to do what pleases him" (Philippians 2:12-13). We are to do our work in obedience, and God will do his work in us so that we might accomplish the mission of spiritual growth.

What, then, are the specifics of "showing the results of our salvation"? In other words, what exactly do we do to grow spiritually?

Volumes have been written on spiritual disciplines. Though we cannot provide an exhaustive list or an exhaustive treatment of each discipline on the list, let's review the most common ways Christians seek to grow in God's power.

One of the most commonly mentioned spiritual disciplines is reading the Bible. After all, if we desire to get our direction from God, there is no better place to look than God's Word. The book of Psalms begins with a majestic call to meditate on the Word of God: "Oh, the joys of those who do not follow the advice of the wicked, or stand around with sinners, or join in with mockers. But they delight in the law of the LORD, meditating on it day and night" (Psalm 1:1-2).

Those who are growing spiritually are not only reading the Word of God regularly, but they are also praying with discipline and persistence. Paul told the church at Ephesus to "pray in the Spirit at all times and on every occasion. Stay alert and be persistent in your prayers for all believers everywhere" (Ephesians 6:18). Again, we are given a plan of action ("pray"), while God's Spirit ("in the Spirit") is our guide and strength.

The writer of Hebrews reminds us that our faithful

participation in the life of our local church will move us toward greater spiritual growth, while also encouraging other believers in the church. He says we should "think of ways to motivate one another to acts of love and good works. And let us not neglect our meeting together, as some people do, but encourage one another, especially now that the day of his return is drawing near" (Hebrews 10:24-25).

The writer was not suggesting that mere attendance was a requisite for church members. The entire context of the book reminds us that our attendance is manifest in small groups, in fellowship, in discipleship, and in ministry to one another. But obviously we cannot be vital participants in those aspects of church life unless we show up.

Someone who is growing as a follower of Christ will also naturally and supernaturally share the gospel with others. As we noted earlier, when Peter and John were told by the authorities to stop talking about Jesus to others, they responded with boldness, "Do you think God wants us to obey you rather than him? We cannot stop telling about everything we have seen and heard" (Acts 4:19-20).

These are some common ways that Christians participate in God's work in order to grow spiritually. It is not an exhaustive list, but it's a good start. Indeed, someone who reads the Bible daily, prays regularly, attends church faithfully, and shares the gospel boldly is likely to be a person on the path to spiritual growth or sanctification.

And the good news is that God gives us everything we need to do these works in his power.

DISCUSSION QUESTIONS

1. In your own words, define *sanctification*.

2. What does it mean to work out our salvation? What is our role, and what is God's role?

3. What steps can you take today to move on a path toward greater spiritual growth?

13

I BELIEVE I AM CALLED TO SHARE THE GOSPEL

I was twenty-four years old, and I had never told anyone about Jesus. For sure, I probably had invited several people to church, but I had never told anyone how they could be saved, how their sins could be forgiven, nor how they could have the assurance they would go to heaven when they died.

Frankly, I don't remember exactly why God led me to Jim. I just could not get my friend off my mind. I was a businessman at the time, and I somehow made a connection with him through my profession. He decided to visit our church, but I had no role in inviting him. Indeed, I was frustrated in some ways when he arrived. He came at his own initiative instead of getting a friendly invitation from someone like me.

Jim was hurting badly. His wife had left him for another man. He loved her deeply and could not understand what had transpired. Jim and I became good friends, and he started attending the men's Bible study group in which I participated.

I knew Jim was not a Christian. His questions and conversations made it clear he had not made a commitment to Christ. I was hoping he would hear and respond to the gospel through the pastor's preaching or a Christian more mature than I. It didn't happen.

With each passing day, the conviction grew within me. I was supposed to tell Jim about Jesus. The mere thought of sharing the gospel caused me to break out in a sweat. Where was Billy Graham when I needed him?

The conviction continued to grow within me. I could no longer rationalize that someone else would share the gospel in my stead. God was calling me to do it.

I called Jim that night and asked him if I could come over to his place. Much to my chagrin at the time, he said yes.

How did I do? Terrible. I was shaking when I arrived. I had dry mouth. The words could barely escape my mouth. Jim could clearly tell I was nervous and offered me water. It probably was one of the poorest presentations of the gospel message ever uttered. I felt like a complete failure.

At least I *thought* I was a failure, until Jim told me he wanted to become a Christian. And he did. That experience, as miserable as it was initially, taught me three important lessons. First, God wants our obedience. Second, he will use us in our weakness. Perhaps he will use us even more in our weakness because we have to depend on him.

The third lesson has been my life path. Every believer is called to share the gospel, even me. The Great Commission is a mandate for all Christians.

THE MANDATE OF EVANGELISM

Perhaps the most common passage used to affirm the importance of evangelism is the Great Commission in Matthew 28:18-20: "Jesus came and told his disciples, 'I have been given all authority in heaven and on earth. Therefore, go and make disciples of all the nations, baptizing them in the name of the Father and the Son and the Holy Spirit. Teach these new disciples to obey all the commands I have given you. And be sure of this: I am with you always, even to the end of the age.'"

The beauty of the Great Commission is that it captures the three key components of evangelism. First, we have the joy of knowing that when we obediently share the gospel, we do so in Jesus' power and authority. Second, we are to make disciples; that is, we are to tell people the good news about Jesus so that they may become his followers. Third, we are to help new believers become more devout followers of Christ, beginning with baptism and continuing with the teachings of Jesus.

Though I made a big deal about my nervousness in

sharing the gospel with Jim, my travails pale in comparison to others who have given their hearts, and even their lives, to tell others about Jesus. The apostle Paul wrote to Timothy about the cost of sharing the gospel.

> Always remember that Jesus Christ, a descendent of King David, was raised from the dead. This is the Good News I preach. And because I preach this Good News, I am suffering and have been chained like a criminal. But the word of God cannot be chained. So I am willing to endure anything if it will bring salvation and eternal glory in Christ Jesus to those God has chosen.
>
> 2 TIMOTHY 2:8-10

Shortly after Jesus ascended to heaven and the early church was born, disciples Peter and John found themselves in trouble for telling people about Jesus. They were arrested, put in jail, and ordered to appear before "the council of all the rulers and elders and teachers of religious law" (Acts 4:5).

The two leaders were asked to speak before the council. With that opportunity, Peter and John spoke without hesitation that Jesus was the only way of salvation when they exclaimed, "There is salvation in no one else! God has given no other name under heaven by which we must be saved" (Acts 4:12).

Given one last chance to refrain from speaking about Jesus

before facing further punishment, Peter and John responded, "We cannot stop telling about everything we have seen and heard" (Acts 4:20).

Evangelism is a mandate for all Christians. And sharing the gospel may come with a cost.

THE MESSAGE OF THE GOSPEL

Romans 3:23 is one of the best-known verses in the Bible: "Everyone has sinned; we all fall short of God's glorious standard." It is Paul's powerful reminder to everyone that we are all sinners; no one comes close to the glory of God.

When we sin, we fracture our relationship with a holy and perfect God. In essence, we have told God we will not obey him; we will not submit to his authority. When we sin, we rebel against our perfect God.

The Bible is clear. We all have sinned. We all have fallen short of God's glory. We all deserve to be separated from God for eternity. We all deserve God's wrath.

Yes, we deserve it. But God has made a provision for us to be saved from this eternal judgment.

God sent his one and only Son to take the punishment for us.

His name is Jesus.

Jesus' mission was clear. It was announced by the angel Gabriel when Mary was pregnant: "She will have a son, and you are to name him Jesus, for he will save his people from their sins" (Matthew 1:21).

Apart from Jesus, our predicament is clear. We have sinned and deserve eternal punishment. We have chosen to disobey God. We have spit in the face of a holy God and said we are going our own way. We are sinners. We have rejected him and deserve to be separated from him for eternity.

What if we got what we deserved? What if we had to pay the price for our sins? What if God did not become human and dwell among us? What if Jesus had not died on the cross and taken our punishment? What if he decided he did not want to take our sins upon himself and bear the wrath of God on our behalf?

The Good News, the gospel, is that we don't have to dwell on the "what ifs." Jesus is God in the flesh: "The Word became human and made his home among us. He was full of unfailing love and faithfulness. And we have seen his glory, the glory of the Father's one and only Son" (John 1:14). And Jesus *did* go to the cross. He did take our sins upon himself. He did bear the wrath of God on our behalf. He was our substitute on the cross. He did take our place: "For God made Christ, who never sinned, to be the offering for our sin, so that we could be made right with God through Christ" (2 Corinthians 5:21).

When Jesus hung on the awful cross, he was taking the punishment I deserve. He was taking the punishment you deserve. Like the sacrificial lambs in the Old Testament, the perfect Lamb of God was sacrificed on our behalf. Jesus took the wrath of God onto himself. When the sin of the world was cast upon him, his own Father could not look at him. God the Father turned away.

Darkness fell on the land. "At about three o'clock, Jesus called out with a loud voice, '*Eli, Eli, lema sabachthani?*' which means 'My God, my God, why have you abandoned me?'" (Matthew 27:46).

He who was not sin became sin for me. For you. For the world.

We do not have to ask, "What if?" There is no need for such questions. All the answers have been given in Jesus. He is our Savior.

But we know the story did not end on the cross. Jesus died on the cross. His body was taken and placed securely in a borrowed tomb. A massive rock was rolled across the doorway to secure the tomb. And then, three days later, Jesus rose from the dead. He not only defeated sin; he defeated death.

"Then the angel spoke to the women. 'Don't be afraid!' he said. 'I know you are looking for Jesus, who was crucified. He isn't here! He is risen from the dead, just as he said would happen. Come, see where his body was lying'" (Matthew 28:5-6).

That's the gospel, the Good News. Jesus died for our sins.

That's the gospel, the Good News. Jesus rose from the dead.

That's the gospel, the Good News. Because he lives, so can we.

OUR RESPONSE: REPENTANCE AND FAITH

John the Baptist told them. He reminded them again and again that someone was coming who was much greater than he. Waiting with anticipation for the arrival of Jesus, John baptized many as he proclaimed the coming Messiah.

Then John had the incredible privilege of baptizing the Savior of whom he had spoken. After the baptism, Jesus went into the wilderness for forty days, where he was tempted by Satan and protected by angels.

It was time. It was time for Jesus to begin his mission on earth. So he went into Galilee and preached a message succinctly recorded in the gospel of Mark: "'The time promised by God has come at last!' he announced. 'The Kingdom of God is near! Repent of your sins and believe the Good News!'" (Mark 1:15).

Repent and *believe*. The call for our response is simple in its brevity and profound in its meaning. We must repent. Repentance is turning away from sin. It is not a mere apology for our sin. I have heard too many "apologies" like this one: "I would like to apologize to anyone I may have offended." When I hear such unapologetic apologies, I cringe.

Repentance is so much more than just an apology. Where a sincere apology is asking for forgiveness for a single deed, repentance is a statement of offending a holy God and declaring that you will turn in another direction. When Paul appeared before King Agrippa, he made the meaning of repentance vividly clear: "I preached first to those in Damascus, then in Jerusalem and throughout all Judea, and also to the Gentiles, that all must repent of their sins and turn to God—and prove they have changed by the good things they do" (Acts 26:20).

Paul declares repentance and faith ("turn to God") in the same breath. And he explains that true repentance will result in a changed life. In repentance, you declare that you were walking away from God, but now you are doing an about-face and moving toward God.

Many times I have heard testimonies from Christians who say that, at some point in their lives, they accepted Jesus as their Savior and became a Christian. But later, they explain, they accepted Jesus as Lord.

But it doesn't work that way. You cannot separate Jesus as Savior from Jesus as Lord. If we are true believers, we have by faith believed Christ to be the Savior of the world and our lives. But we have also repented and turned away from sin to confess Jesus as our Lord. Becoming a Christian is not steps A and B. It is repentance and faith together. They are two sides of the same coin.

Faith is believing that Jesus died for your sins, that he rose from the dead, and that he will forgive you and give you eternal life. Faith is not believing a fairy tale you can't prove. It is trusting what Christ has done, rooted in both history and eternity. Though we don't see Christ visibly today, we trust unwaveringly that he is God and that he came as a man and lived among us. Hebrews 11:1 says it powerfully: "Faith shows the reality of what we hope for; it is the evidence of things we cannot see."

One day we will stand before God at the judgment. As Christians, what will be our plea as to why God should allow us into his presence? True Christians know they have done nothing to earn salvation. They know that, apart from Christ, they have no righteousness at all. And they know they responded to the gospel by faith alone. They repented of their sins. And they were made right by the blood of Christ, which was shed on the cross.

Such is the message we must convey to those who are not Christians.

All have sinned. God gave his only Son to save us. We must repent of our sins. We must place our faith in Christ.

We can't help but tell others what we have seen and heard.

I believe in sharing the gospel.

DISCUSSION QUESTIONS

1. Why do you think most Christians hesitate to tell others about Jesus?

2. Why will many people reject Christ and the message of the gospel?

3. What are the essential biblical truths of the gospel?

14

I BELIEVE CHRIST
WILL RETURN

Two days before I wrote this chapter, I was in a meeting with a pastor I coach. We are working together to get his church more outwardly focused and seeking prayerfully how to reach more people with the gospel. At the beginning of our meeting, he said with a grin on his face, "Thom, I discovered how to grow my church." He could see the curiosity on my face, so he responded quickly. "Teach a series of lessons on the return of Christ or the book of Revelation."

He told me how his church had placed a simple ad on social media: "Hear Pastor Jim teach on the return of Christ for the next five Sundays."

"I am in week two of the series," Jim told me. "Our

attendance is up 20 percent. Now I've got to figure out how to keep all these people."

Though my friend found a bit of humor in the unexpected surge in attendance, his experience is not that unusual. There is a definitive interest in the end times. The level of interest has ebbed and flowed over the past several decades, but it still intrigues people. Perhaps they want to know the end of the story. Perhaps they are looking for some hope in this messed-up world. Perhaps they are just curiosity seekers.

When I was pastor of a church in St. Petersburg, Florida, a group of people from the neighborhood all showed up together at our worship service. I soon learned they were following the teachings of a man who had convinced them that Christ would return in less than two months. They wanted to know if they were welcome in my church. While I welcomed them to worship with us, I respectfully asked that they not recruit people in the church and try to convince them of a specific end-times date.

Of course, the date of certitude came and nothing happened. Jesus did not meet their deadline. Those families soon stopped attending our church.

We must approach the issue of Christ's return with both expectancy and humility. We anticipate his return with great excitement. But we hold loosely such matters as the exact timing. We focus on those things that we can definitively glean from Scripture.

THE EVENTS THAT PRECEDE THE RETURN OF CHRIST

The Bible identifies a number of events that will precede the return of Christ. Let's look at some of them specifically from Matthew 24 (though passages in the other three Gospels also point to Christ's return). In Matthew, Jesus' disciples want to know about his return as well. They ask him, "Tell us, when will all this happen? What sign will signal your return and the end of the world?" (Matthew 24:3).

Wars and threats of more wars. Jesus told his disciples, "Don't let anyone mislead you, for many will come in my name, claiming, 'I am the Messiah.' They will deceive many. And you will hear of wars and threats of wars, but don't panic. Yes, these things must take place, but the end won't follow immediately" (Matthew 24:4-6).

Famines and earthquakes. Again, Jesus tells his disciples that these catastrophes will happen, "but all this is only the first of the birth pains, with more to come" (Matthew 24:8).

Widespread persecution of Christians. The persecution of Christians is a common theme of the end times in the Bible. Jesus tells his followers, "You will be arrested, persecuted, and killed. You will be hated all over the world because you are my followers" (Matthew 24:9).

Unprecedented astronomical phenomena. Jesus seems to be saying that these events will immediately precede his return. He describes how "the sun will be darkened, the moon will give no light, the stars will fall from the sky, and the powers in the heavens will be shaken" (Matthew 24:29).

Matthew 24 offers a vivid picture of the events leading up to the return of Christ. The importance of the words is heightened because they came from the mouth of Jesus. But there are many more passages of Scripture dealing with the end times. For example, Paul describes a "man of lawlessness" (2 Thessalonians 2:8) who will wreak havoc before Jesus returns. His role will be to "do the work of Satan. . . . He will use every kind of evil deception to fool those on their way to destruction, because they refuse to love and accept the truth that would save them" (2 Thessalonians 2:9-10). In other words, the man of lawlessness will work evil to try to keep lost people from getting saved.

THE CHALLENGE OF TIMING

It is clear that Christ's return will be a most magnificent event. No one will be able to deny that moment. Paul says, "The Lord himself will come down from heaven with a commanding shout, with the voice of the archangel, and with the trumpet call of God" (1 Thessalonians 4:16).

But we cannot know the precise timing of his return. Just moments before his ascension into heaven, Jesus told his followers, "The Father alone has the authority to set those dates and times, and they are not for you to know" (Acts 1:7).

The entirety of Revelation 20 focuses on the events before, during, and after the "thousand years" (see Revelation 20:1-7 in particular). Many have debated the precise meaning of this period, typically called the Millennium. One view, called the *amillennial* view, holds that we are presently in the Millennium. That is, it is the present church age, beginning right after Christ's resurrection and ascension. It is thus not a literal thousand years, but a figure of speech to represent a long period.

The *postmillennial* view holds that Jesus will actually return after the one thousand years noted in Revelation 2:4-5. Thus, Jesus returns *after* the Millennium. His reign will begin after the Millennium as well. Even within this view, some believe the Millennium is a literal one thousand years; others do not.

The *premillennial* view holds that Christ will return *before* the Millennium. His return will be sudden and mostly unexpected. According to this view, Christ will then reign in a period of peace and righteousness over the earth. Satan and his demons will be removed from the earth:

> Then I saw an angel coming down from heaven
> with the key to the bottomless pit and a heavy chain
> in his hand. He seized the dragon—that old serpent,
> who is the devil, Satan—and bound him in chains
> for a thousand years. The angel threw him into the

bottomless pit, which he then shut and locked so
Satan could not deceive the nations anymore until
the thousand years were finished. Afterward he must
be released for a little while.

REVELATION 20:1-3

These three views represent divergent views of the
Millennium, but they do not even begin to cover all the
related issues that are discussed and debated. There seems to
be an insatiable appetite to understand the mysterious language of the book of Revelation and other end-times passages.

WHAT WE KNOW

Though we must accept the mystery of many aspects of
the second coming of Jesus and events surrounding the end
times, there still is much we can know. Let's look at some key
issues that are clear in the Bible.

Jesus will return. Though we may not agree on the timing
and specifics surrounding his return, we can affirm that Jesus
will indeed come back. Some aspects of Jesus' return are mentioned in twenty-three of the twenty-seven New Testament
books. Shortly after Jesus ascended to heaven, the two angels
(white-robed men) told his followers he would return just as
he left: "'Men of Galilee,' they said, 'why are you standing
here staring into heaven? Jesus has been taken from you into

heaven, but someday he will return from heaven in the same way you saw him go!'" (Acts 1:11). The language leaves no doubt that Jesus will literally return.

The words of the angels follow a similar theme that runs throughout the New Testament. Jesus will return. The angels are emphatic about that. But the angels do not provide specificity on the timing of Christ's return. It will simply be *someday*.

The importance of the Second Coming is certainly confirmed by its pervasiveness in Scripture. The confessions of the early church also affirm its importance. The Apostles' Creed says that Jesus will return "to judge the living and the dead." The Nicene Creed similarly says that Jesus "will come again in glory to judge the living and the dead and his kingdom will have no end." (See both confessions in the appendix.)

Christians should be both expectant and excited about Christ's return. The Bible is clear that all believers should look forward to the return of Jesus. Though some troublesome issues are evident in the complete narrative of the end times, Jesus' return is a time of victory and celebration for all believers.

The Bible refers to Jesus as the bridegroom and the church as the bride of Christ (see Ephesians 5:25-27). The return of Christ is, therefore, the reunion of the bride and the bridegroom. As the bride of Christ, believers wait with anticipation and joy for the time when we will see the bride-groom face-to-face.

Christ's second coming will be different from his first coming. In his first coming, Jesus was a baby born in a stable in Bethlehem. He lived a humble and meek life on earth. Whereas humility marked his first coming, glory will be the mark of his second coming. Paul writes, "The Lord himself will come down from heaven with a commanding shout, with the voice of the archangel, and with the trumpet call of God" (1 Thessalonians 4:16).

Christ's second coming will be a time of hope for believers but a time of dread for those who do not believe. Though Scripture points to the agony and fate of unbelievers, we are assured that believers should have great hope. When Paul wrote to the church in Thessalonica, he reminded the believers there that "God chose to save us through our Lord Jesus Christ, not to pour out his anger on us. Christ died for us so that, whether we are dead or alive when he returns, we can live with him forever. So encourage each other and build each other up, just as you are already doing" (1 Thessalonians 5:9-11).

Christ's return will be visible and final. Recall from our earlier discussion that the angels told those who witnessed Christ's ascension that "Jesus has been taken from you into heaven, but someday he will return from heaven in the same way you saw him go!" (Acts 1:11). Just as they *saw* Jesus ascend, they will *see* him return. Jesus told his followers similarly, that "they will *see* the Son of Man coming on the clouds of heaven with power and great glory" (Matthew 24:30, italics added).

Christ's return will be the culmination of history. Peter provides the reason why Christ has not returned to reign before now: "The Lord isn't really being slow about his promise, as some people think. No, he is being patient for your sake. He does not want anyone to be destroyed, but wants everyone to repent" (2 Peter 3:9).

Amazingly, the fact that Christ has not yet come to render his final judgment is another affirmation of his love. He desires that none should perish, but that all should embrace Christ as their Savior and Lord.

Ultimately though, Christ's return will come suddenly. "The day of the Lord," says Peter, "will come as unexpectedly as a thief. Then the heavens will pass away with a terrible noise, and the very elements themselves will disappear in fire, and the earth and everything on it will be found to deserve judgment" (2 Peter 3:10).

But even that horrific scene of judgment is not something Christians should fear or dread. Believers, instead, "are looking forward to the new heavens and new earth he has promised, a world filled with God's righteousness" (2 Peter 3:13).

Thus we wait with expectation and hope.

"He who is the faithful witness to all these things says, 'Yes, I am coming soon!'

Amen! Come, Lord Jesus!" (Revelation 22:20).

DISCUSSION QUESTIONS

1. What are some of the events that will precede the return of Christ?

2. What are the three perspectives on the Millennium?

3. Though Christians do not always agree on certain specifics of Christ's return, what are some truths about his return that are undeniable in Scripture?

15

I BELIEVE IN HEAVEN

Sometime in our lives, we all experience the death of a loved one. For some, the times of grief come early in life. For others, it is later. I have a friend whose parents did not die until he was in his sixties.

When my dad died, I experienced deep grief for the first time in my life. I was only in my twenties. Dad's cancer diagnosis and his death took place in about a two-month period. My world was shaken. I was, however, greatly comforted that my dad was a Christian. My pain was deep, but my hope was real. I knew beyond a doubt my father was with his heavenly Father. And I knew I would see my dad again.

Heaven is a real place. Heaven is a place of hope for believers in Christ. Though we don't become angels or get angel wings as popular culture sometimes tells us, we do get to be with Christ. We do have the joy of eternal life.

Sometimes the topics of final judgment and hell are included in conversations of eternity. Let's look at those two and then resume our discussion of heaven.

THE FINAL JUDGMENT

The final judgment is for everyone, believers and non-believers alike. We learn in Acts 10:42 that "Jesus is the one appointed by God to be the judge of all—the living and the dead." For believers, the time of judgment is not a time when their eternal destination will be determined. That took place when they repented of their sins and placed their faith in Christ.

Believers in Christ "will all stand before the judgment seat of God" (Romans 14:10). Paul goes on to say, "Yes, each of us will give a personal account to God. So let's stop condemning each other. Decide instead to live in such a way that you will not cause another believer to stumble and fall" (Romans 14:12-13). The judgment for Christians will be an accounting of our lives on earth. Paul writes, "Whether we are here in this body or away from this body, our goal is to please him. For we must all stand before Christ to be judged. We will each receive whatever we deserve for the good or evil we have done in this earthly body" (2 Corinthians 5:9-10).

We believers, then, will be rewarded for the good we have done, and the evil we have done will be blotted out by Christ's death on the cross. The stated verdict for our sins will be: *forgiven*. Though there will be some type of acknowledgement or reward for our good works, every believer's joy in heaven will be perfect and complete.

Unbelievers, however, will face a dramatically different final judgment. God "will pour out his anger and wrath on those who live for themselves, who refuse to obey the truth and instead live lives of wickedness" (Romans 2:8). The final judgment is, as its name indicates, final. There is no second chance, no reincarnation, and no purgatory. For believers and unbelievers alike, Christ's judgment and verdict will be complete at the final judgment.

HELL

Every time I read about hell in the Bible, I feel an enormous burden and sadness. It can be a part of the Bible that I look over quickly lest I get overwhelmed at the fate of those who do not believe. Some Christians have actually moved their doctrinal position to believe that death for non-Christians is simply ceasing to exist. That belief is called annihilationism. When we die, we no longer have an existence.

Though such a belief may seem more palatable for us than an eternal hell, it is not taught in Scripture. Humans are eternal creatures and will not cease to exist after death. At the final judgment, those who have not become followers of Christ will go to a place of eternal punishment called hell.

Jesus was very clear in his statements about hell. Speaking of those who are not believers, he said, "The King will turn to those on the left and say, 'Away with you, you cursed ones, into the eternal fire prepared for the devil and his demons'" (Matthew 25:41). Jesus then emphasized that the lost and the saved will go in two different directions: "They will go away into eternal punishment, but the righteous will go into eternal life" (Matthew 25:46).

In chapter 13, we took a brief excursion into the mandate to evangelize, to share the gospel with others. We certainly should be obedient to that command because it comes directly from Jesus. When we are not seeking to be evangelistic, we are by default being disobedient. Another motive for evangelism is to share with nonbelievers the opportunity to receive the presence of God in their lives today, and then to be with God forever in heaven.

But our motivation should also include a profound, compassionate concern that no one should perish and go into an eternity without Christ. We should feel compelled to share the Good News because it is indeed good news. We should also feel compelled to share the Good News because the alternative is very bad news.

If we don't go to heaven, we will go to hell. And if we

don't go to hell, we will go to heaven. There are only two paths. Let us look now at the path that leads to heaven.

HEAVEN

God currently dwells in heaven. When Jesus taught his disciples to pray, he said, "Our Father in heaven, may your name be kept holy" (Matthew 6:9). When Jesus ascended, the two men in white told the disciples that "Jesus has been taken from you into heaven, but someday he will return from heaven in the same way you saw him go!" (Acts 1:11). Heaven is the current home of God the Father and Jesus. God is in heaven, but he is also everywhere (omnipresent). Still, God's power and blessings are most clearly seen in heaven, where everyone worships him.

The word *heaven* is often used as a basic term for where all believers will spend eternity. There is certainly nothing wrong with that understanding. But it seems as if most conversations about heaven include little discussion of the new heavens and new earth. Yet, Isaiah spoke prophetically about this coming age:

"As surely as my new heavens and earth will remain,
so will you always be my people, with a name that
will never disappear," says the LORD.

ISAIAH 66:22

When Christ returns, he will reign over the new heavens and new earth. The current heavens and earth will disappear to yield to this place called the new Jerusalem in the book of Revelation. John vividly describes a vision of this new reality in Revelation 21:1-2:

> I saw a new heaven and a new earth, for the old heaven and the old earth had disappeared. And the sea was also gone. And I saw the holy city, the new Jerusalem, coming down from God out of heaven like a bride beautifully dressed for her husband.

John's vision continues with unambiguous clarity that God will dwell with us in this new home. John says that he "heard a loud shout from the throne, saying, 'Look, God's home is now among his people! He will live with them, and they will be his people. God himself will be with them'" (Revelation 21:3). Heaven will become the new heaven and the new earth. It will be the home of believers forever. What, then, will heaven be like?

WHAT WILL HEAVEN BE LIKE?

Though this brief discussion cannot begin to cover the main themes of our future life in heaven, let's look at some of the more common points. Clearly, heaven is a place of incalculable joy and blessings.

There will be no pain or sorrow. It is a cliché to say, "Life is tough," but it is nevertheless true. During our finite lives, we experience physical and emotional pain. We go through periods of sorrow. We may struggle with hopelessness. We have relational conflicts and misunderstandings. But all of that will disappear in heaven. God "will wipe every tear from their eyes, and there will be no more death or sorrow or crying or pain. All these things are gone forever" (Revelation 21:4).

Christians often say they don't look forward to dying, but they look forward to life after death. In other words, the process of dying can mean pain and struggle, but the other side of dying is eternal life, when believers will be with Christ forever. Among the reasons for such anticipation is the prospect of freedom from pain and suffering. Heaven is indeed a wonderful place.

We will not become angels. As noted earlier, we do not become angels when we die. Angels and humans are two distinct creations of God. Paul writes, "I'm torn between two desires: I long to go and be with Christ, which would be far better for me. But for your sakes, it is better that I continue to live" (Philippians 1:23-24). Paul speaks of his same personhood ("I") whether he speaks of being on earth or in heaven. When we die, we will not change our identities, but we will change our location.

We will have emotions of laughter and joy. You may have heard the cynical comment that heaven seems like a boring place. That we will either be playing a harp or singing. In truth, heaven is the antithesis of boring. There is singing, but joyous singing. There are celebrations and banquets. Jesus even spoke of laughter in heaven: "God blesses you who weep now, for in due time you will laugh" (Luke 6:21).

We will have glorified bodies. Of course, many of us would like to know exactly what a glorified body is like. We can only speculate when we talk about bodies of great speed or the ability to fly. It is better that we affirm what the Bible teaches. We will have bodies free of pain, disease, and limitations. The crippled will walk. The blind will see. The deaf will hear. The mute will speak.

We will recognize each other. We can learn a lot about heaven from reading about Christ's resurrected body. For example, he was recognized by many in his resurrected body. His disciples recognized him (see John 20 and 21). In 1 Corinthians 15:5-8, Paul notes all the different people who recognized Jesus after his resurrection:

He was seen by Peter and then by the Twelve.
After that, he was seen by more than 500 of his

followers at one time, most of whom are still alive, though some have died. Then he was seen by James and later by all the apostles. Last of all, as though I had been born at the wrong time, I also saw him.

Similarly, Christ's disciples recognized the glorified bodies of Moses and Elijah in the transfiguration of Christ (Luke 9:29-33). They had different and better bodies, but they were still identifiable as Moses and Elijah.

There are many other aspects of heaven we could address, and they would all be matters of joy and celebration. I recently celebrated Christmas with eighteen Rainers, including my wife, my sons, my sons' wives, and my grandchildren. It was hectic, disorganized, and often loud. But through it all, I saw incalculable joy, laughter, and fun.

It was tempting for me to think such great moments could not be surpassed. But I know they will.

I believe the Bible.

I believe in Jesus.

I believe in heaven.

And I believe that all my fellow believers and I will be in heaven together in the blink of an eye. It will be the most joyous time ever.

Even more, it will be the most joyous time *forever*.

DISCUSSION QUESTIONS

1. How is the final judgment a time for everyone, both believers and nonbelievers?

2. Why should the doctrines of heaven and hell compel us to share the gospel with others?

3. What are some aspects of heaven we can affirm from the Bible? In other words, what will heaven be like?

APPENDIX

Two of the earliest confessions of faith in the church were the Apostles' Creed and the Nicene Creed. Both were established during the first four centuries of the church. One of their primary purposes was to refute incipient doctrinal heresies. Additionally, though, they became a good gauge of how doctrine had developed in the church. You will note that many of the issues addressed in these creeds are still relevant and accurate today. They should be both relevant and accurate because they are faithful to Scripture.

The creeds were only slightly changed to reflect our common description of the third person of the Trinity. So "Holy Ghost" became "Holy Spirit." It could be a helpful exercise to look at the two creeds and compare them to some of the doctrines in this book.

THE APOSTLES' CREED

I believe in God,
the Father almighty,
Creator of heaven and earth,
and in Jesus Christ, his only Son, our Lord,
who was conceived by the Holy Spirit,
born of the Virgin Mary,
suffered under Pontius Pilate,
was crucified, died, and was buried;
he descended into hell;
on the third day he rose again from the dead;
he ascended into heaven,
and is seated at the right hand of God the Father almighty;
from there he will come to judge the living and the dead.

I believe in the Holy Spirit,
the holy catholic Church,
the communion of saints,
the forgiveness of sins,
the resurrection of the body,
and the life everlasting. Amen.

THE NICENE CREED

I believe in one God,
the Father almighty,
Maker of heaven and earth,
of all things visible and invisible.

I believe in one Lord Jesus Christ,
the Only Begotten Son of God,
born of the Father before all ages.
God from God, Light from Light,
true God from true God,
begotten, not made, consubstantial with the Father;
through him all things were made.
For us men and for our salvation
he came down from heaven,
and by the Holy Spirit was incarnate of the Virgin Mary,
and became man.
For our sake he was crucified under Pontius Pilate,
he suffered death and was buried,
and rose again on the third day
in accordance with the Scriptures.
He ascended into heaven
and is seated at the right hand of the Father.
He will come again in glory

to judge the living and the dead
and his kingdom will have no end.

I believe in the Holy Spirit, the Lord, the giver of life,
who proceeds from the Father and the Son,
who with the Father and the Son is adored and glorified,
who has spoken through the prophets.

I believe in one, holy, catholic, and apostolic Church.
I confess one Baptism for the forgiveness of sins
and I look forward to the resurrection of the dead
and the life of the world to come. Amen.

NOTES

1. Adapted from Paul Enns, *The Moody Handbook of Theology* (Chicago: Moody, 2008), 173.
2. Adapted from Enns, 174–175.
3. See, for example, "The 50 Most Popular and Read Bible Verses," Bible Study Tools, August 30, 2021, https://www.biblestudytools .com/topical-verses/the-25-most-read-bible-verses/.

ABOUT THE AUTHOR

THOM S. RAINER is the founder and CEO of Church Answers. With nearly forty years of ministry experience, Thom has spent a lifetime committed to the growth and health of the local church and its leaders. He has been a pastor of four churches and interim pastor of ten churches, as well as a bestselling author, popular speaker, professor, and dean. He is a 1977 graduate of the University of Alabama and earned his MDiv and PhD degrees from The Southern Baptist Theological Seminary. Rainer has written numerous books, including three that ranked as number one bestsellers: *I Am a Church Member*, *Autopsy of a Deceased Church*, and *Simple Church*. He and his wife live in Franklin, Tennessee.

DISCOVER WHAT IT REALLY MEANS TO BE A CHRISTIAN

Pastor, author, and church consultant Thom Rainer explains how you can find your true purpose within the community of fellow believers at your local church.

I Am a Christian: What does it really mean to be a Christian? In a world where everything from sports to politics, social media to podcasts, and movies to television competes for our attention, we need to get back to what is essential. When we finally grasp who we are in Christ and what our participation means to the local church, everything changes. Life begins to make sense. Our purpose becomes clear. Our mission through the local church is confirmed. Our hearts start longing to cooperate with God in the company of fellow believers.

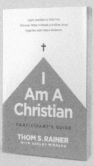

I Am a Christian Participant's Guide: This eight-week guide is designed to accompany Thom Rainer's *I Am a Christian DVD Experience*. Created for group or individual use.

I Am a Christian DVD Experience: In this eight-week video experience, Thom Rainer will help you and your small group dig deeper into what it really means to be a Christian and how your life will bloom when it's rooted in the local church. CP1787

If you liked this book, you'll want to get involved in

Church Equip!

Do you have a desire to learn more about serving God through your local church?

Would you like to see how God can use you in new and exciting ways?

Get your church involved in Church Equip, an online ministry designed to prepare church leaders and church members to better serve God's mission and purpose.

Check us out at **ChurchEquip.com**

On the Prologue and Act One Kitchen

The design is a series of reveals that play with the expectations of an audience who either thought they were coming to a cabaret show or a 'serious play' at the theatre. The middle-class kitchen is revealed behind a bright green theatrical festoon-swagged curtain that provides a backdrop to the prologue. There is a long history of kitchen sink drama at the Royal Court Theatre going right back to *Look Back in Anger* and we wanted to draw on that lineage with an entirely naturalistic box set for the first act, complete with working sink and kettle.

The Prologue

Act One: Kitchen

Act One: The Play – 'Today Is The Day'

The play should be performed serious. Sharp. Staccato. Although there may be a strong sense of irony within it, the cast are wanting to put on this play. They are proud of it. Despite its limitations. They are in on the joke, but they don't play the joke.

The curtain opens to reveal the set for Today Is The Day. *Imagine a crisp, white, European edgy kitchen set. Like something that has been on this stage before. Sharp lines, cool, and slick. The kitchen has a table with chairs around it, a kettle, and a large clock. Maybe three different types of clocks.*

Also in the set is a glass 'green room'. This is a see-through box that acts as the cast's visible backstage – and the sound box. Here, the cast can make the live sounds for the play, sew outfits, retouch make-up, fan themselves, roll cigs, have a drink, read their script, rest. It is to show the workings.

Right now, as the curtain opens, all the cast are in this green room, quickly changing from their previous outfit into Act One attire, which is kind of a modern theatre style 'ensemble' costume. Think beige. Grey, neutral tones, COS-style aesthetic, trousers with a drop line. This should contrast with the performers' painted faces.

We see **Ms Sharon** *look at the clock and start a metronome inside the green room – which starts the ticking of the clock.*

Rhys *walks in, on the phone, looking busy and preoccupied.*

Rhys   No, no, I can't do the gig tonight, I told you. I'm uh… Well I'm busy. I told you this weeks ago. Well, find another girl then, if there's so many of us, I fucking quit anyway!

Rhys *hangs up and throws the phone away. Distressed.* **Sadie** *walks in.*

Sadie   Quitting what?

Rhys   Oh, Sadie, I –

Sadie   You can't just quit, Rhys. What else are you gunna do?

Rhys   I can do lots of things actually. Loads. Tonnes. The list goes on and on.

Sadie   Right. We all think about quitting Rhys, but you know you speak like that to an employer –

Rhys   You were listening to my call?

Sadie   You speak through a permanent megaphone. All of Sloane Square were listening to your call…

Rhys   If you're coming here to make things worse then just go –

Sadie   I'm sorry. It's just the stress of everything, of today, of doing this. It's scary.

They sit down.
They wait.
Rhys *goes to speak but* **Sadie** *raises a hand as if to silence.*

Sadie   They can wait.

Rhys   Absolutely.

The clock ticks.

Rhys   Queer time, it's a whole other concept.

Sadie   Plus we're… (*gestures to their skin*)

Rhys   Yeah I mean

Sadie   gotta be intersectional

Rhys   means we can be *very* late

Sadie   definitely

Rhys   absolutely

Sadie   quite right.

Rhys   Cuppa, Sadie?

Sadie   Hm?

Rhys   Tea?

Sadie   I don't have any to spill.

Rhys   Go on, it will calm your nerves.

Rhys *gets up to turn on the kettle.* **Ms Sharon** *makes the noise of the kettle, maybe by whistling. We see* **Sue** *and another cast member join in the whistling to harmonise.*

Rhys *makes a cup of tea for* **Sadie**, *genuinely, and a glass of water with two ice cubes (handed to him by* **Midgitte** *through the green room seamlessly) into water.*

Sadie   You normally love your tea.

Rhys   Love? Bit strong, I like tea.

Sadie   Okay, you normally *like* your tea.

Rhys   You can have too much of it, it's hard to focus.

Sadie   Right.

Rhys   We need focus, today of all days.

Sadie   You're right Rhys, of all the days, today, we really do need to focus.

Rhys   Uh, right, yes. You think the others will come?

Sadie   I think so, they were at the RVT earlier today, it's not far by train.

Rhys   Well last weekend, I bumped into a train driver in a dark room at the sauna, we were both in quite a compromising position, like Twister, but right at the very end, so I struck up a conversation, and in that conversation, he mentioned in passing a strike coming up, may affect their journey.

Sadie   They have the news app, I'm sure they can find a way.

Rhys   In fact, in that same dark room in the sauna last weekend, I met a postman, and he said some interesting things about unions.

Sadie   Union chat, in a dark room – a true community space.

Rhys   Well, he said that us throwing a union meeting isn't a bad idea, but just to be prepared for differing opinions. Some people won't like us doing it.

Sadie   When has being liked ever been the goal, if that was the case we would've all stopped singing Katy Perry covers a decade ago.

Rhys   I'm not sure if we are ready.

Sadie   For what?

Rhys   For our first action as a newly formed union to be so… damning.

Sadie   That's the whole reason we unionised in the first place, because of this action, because of what we have decided to do, we can't just –

Rhys   Yes but, to go after someone like –

Sadie *slams the table and dramatically looks at* **Rhys**, *then looks away, then looks back at* **Rhys** *again.*

Sadie   Don't you dare speak his name.

Rhys   I wasn't going to, I was just going to say 'him'.

Sadie   Don't you dare speak his personal pronoun.

Rhys   I, uh –

Sadie   He's cost me jobs –

Rhys   Uh Sadie, you're using *his* personal pronoun.

Sadie   Urgh. They've cost me jobs, affected my livelihood, they're splitting up our family, one member at a time choosing them over us. They just pack up, leave in the middle of the night, to them, to that, to everything that they make people do. You think that isn't worth going after?

Rhys   No, you're right.

Sadie   Jesus, what's gotten into you, someone really has got your corset in a twist.

Rhys   I just didn't think organising a union meeting would feel so…important.

Sadie   So vital?

Rhys   So timely.

Sadie   Necessary.

They wait. The clock ticks.

Sadie   You nervous?

Rhys   About what?

Sadie   This.

Rhys   Look, Sadie, there's a lot going on, do you mean *this* (*points to them in the scene*), or do you mean *this* (*points to like, doing a play in front of people*)?

Sadie   This. The meeting.

Rhys   Yeah, I am. Feels like a big deal.

Sadie   It's all the pauses.

Rhys   What?

Sadie   The pauses. Makes it all feel like a big deal. Everything feels like a big deal when there's a pause.

Rhys   Really?

Sadie   Yeah, look. It's a trick as old as time.

Sadie *clears her throat to demonstrate.*

Sadie   'The drag queen stuck in the machine, only genderfucks on Halloween.'

Sadie *re-positions to try again.*

Sadie   The drag queen…

Sadie *pauses, looks around, looks at the audience, takes a deep breath.*

Sadie   …stuck in the machine
only genderfucks
on Halloween.

Rhys   Fuck, you're right…. Or sorry,
fuck…

Pauses.

Rhys   …you're right.

They both pause. Pondering on that. As **Wet Mess**, **Lilly**, **Sue** *walk in the door.*

Midgitte, **Sharon** *and* **Chiyo** *stay in the green room. Chilling, having a cig.*

Lilly *is on the phone, and she is ushering* **Wet Mess** *to remember the suitcase.*

Lilly (*on the phone*)   Okay sure don't come to the meeting, I'm sorry my big tits and existing vagina stopped me from having no fucking morals.

Drops phone and turns straight to the room sweetly.

Lilly   Hi, sorry I'm late, it's like herding cattle. (*Gestures to* **Wet Mess**.)

As **Wet Mess** *walks in, they do a seamless loop back round to have* **Ms Sharon** *hold out a briefcase from the green room that they forgot, and then they all come down and take a seat.*

Sue   Sorry I'm late, it was really quite the ordeal, there was traffic.

The cast pull out spotlights/makeshift flashlights on **Sue***, signifying a monologue, as the lighting dramatically shifts to only be on* **Sue***.*

Sue   It was yesterday, the day before today and the day after whatever day was before, and I had just finished a gig in the basement of this rich man's house. He was throwing a party for his kid's eighteenth, and they live in this big estate near Hampstead. Well, we met in the Heath in one of my late night excursions, and after we, uh…met, he asked me why I had long nails – I said I do drag and that also I enjoy the glamour of life, rather than the monotony. Anyway he explained to me that he was married, had two kids, and that he loved them very much but every now and again he needed to explore something outside of the castle he had built to feel an ounce something. He said he saw Harry Styles on a magazine whilst drinking a Starbucks coffee that had a rainbow flag on it, and it made him feel like there was a whole other life he could be living. Most of the time he doesn't think it, but when he's doing something that feels so, so, well so straight – he just needs that hit of something else. Anyway, it was his kid's eighteenth and it felt like the epitome of all the bland choices he had made for himself – this heterosexual castle that would not move, Jo Malone perfume seeping deeper and deeper into the collar of his shirt – so he hired me to perform in the basement of his house. He'd sneak down to come and see me, and all I had to do was a lip sync on the hour, every hour, I guess to make him feel alive. He promised to tip me in clothes he had bought for his wife that she did not wear. Well, who can resist Chanel? It was all going well, until I was mid-Cher lip sync, 'Turn Back Time', well he was in front of me shedding one singular tear as one of his hands rubbed his crotch area – when none other than his wife walked in. She was absolutely heartbroken to see the man she loved with a drag queen, even more upset to see him crying to a Cher song, that she started yelling at him. Well he said to her that it wasn't his fault, that I'd kept him there, in his own basement against his will, so she turned on me. She starts trying to hit me with the heel of her Louboutin, now I know if I hit back the papers will have a field day, so I just try to dip and dodge, but a heel did scratch my eye, I manage to escape, leaving all my daytime clothes in the basement – but as I get out onto the road, crying as I wait for my Uber, the one that stops to pick me up, well he sees me and he shouts, 'I'M NOT PICKING UP SOME SINFUL FUCKING DEVIANT YOU'RE GOING TO HELL YOU FAGGOT' and I had to walk all the way here, and, and that is why I'm late.

The spotlights disappear, the lighting resumes, the cast act as if **Sue***'s explanation was short and sharp.*

Sadie   Okay Sue, and you two, why were you late?

Lilly   I actually would've been on time if it wasn't for this one.

Wet Mess   Hey, it's queer time.

Lilly   Right.

Wet Mess   Plus I'm non-binary, time is fluid baby.

Rhys   Tea?

Sue   I have absolutely loads to spill.

Rhys   No, as in, cuppa?

All (*their version of saying yes, and* **Ms Sharon** *in the green room also joins in on the mic going, 'Mmm yesss, yess.'*)

Rhys *goes to turn on the kettle.* **Ms Sharon** *makes the kettle noise again, with* **Midgitte** *and* **Chiyo** *doing a little whistle beat over it, dead serious.*

Rhys *gives everyone tea.*

Rhys   So, today, is the day.

Sadie   It is, today.

Sue   Is it, today?

Lilly   Yeah, it's today.

Wet Mess   It feels like today.

Sue   Good weather for today.

Sadie   Yeah, no clouds, perfect for today.

Lilly   And not much traffic today.

Sue   That's good, today of all days.

Rhys *purposefully drops their tea and saucer on the floor. It smashes. They all look at the same time. The tension is there.*

Rhys   Today, is the day. The day is today. I can feel it. Feel *it* in my heart. In the tingling of my toes. And also, because I checked the calendar. That today is the day. It's weird how a day creeps up on you. Slow but present, present…and slow. Like a snail that is in front of you. Crawling towards you. Like Monday turning to Tuesday to Wednesday, days, changing. Then this day appears. And you think to yourself: *it is today, isn't it?*

Rhys *holds the pause. Then returns to the table.*

Rhys   You think the others will come?

Lilly   I shouldn't bet on it. I could tell there was nerves.

Sue   They might just be late.

Wet Mess   Yeah, fluid time babyyy.

Sadie   And Midgitte is a live performance artist – so that's like… really late.

Rhys   Well, we could start without them, the meeting that is, about the mission. We won't start the mission, but maybe just summarise our notes.

Lilly   We must do it all together, it's all or nothing, what's a first union meeting if only half of us are here – what is it we read in that manual?

Rhys   Fragmented action equals fragmented outcome.

Lilly   Exactly. And I'm not risking all this for a fragmented outcome.

They pause, they notice the clock ticking again.

Sue   Can someone stop the fucking clock tick.

Sharon *stops the metronome.*

Sue   Sorry, I'm just tense. Just never thought we'd follow through.

Lilly   Where is everyone, thought there'd be loads of us?

Wet Mess   There's a three-day photoshoot happening for a new Amazon Prime campaign, they wanted drag queens in it – so a lot of people are just busy. Tag line was something like, 'slayed at werk'.

Sue   It's ridiculous.

Sadie   I mean what was the buy-out? Cus I can do a lot of ridiculous shit for 30k.

Wet Mess   I'll show you the buy-out…

Wet Mess *mimes sucking off Jeff Bezos with money spurting out.*

Rhys   Sucking off Jeff Bezos, not a great excuse.

Sadie   Better than sucking off Steve Jobs, at least Bezos is alive.

Lilly   Glamazon Prime!!!

Sue   What?

Lilly   Potential drag names. That one is for when eventually all drag is ran by Amazon, who after twenty years of buying out all the gay clubs and turning them into Amazon Hubs, realise a way to cut down costs is get rid of the clubs altogether. Drag is streamed virtually into your homes, and you're allowed to pick one last lip sync before your house is ruined and submerged underwater because the climate crisis caused floods.

Rhys   Truly a lip sync for your life.

They all laugh except **Sue**.

Sadie   You okay?

Sue   Yeah, just, wild to think that by tomorrow it may all be… Done, that –

Lilly   Don't say his name.

Sue   – that, *he*, might not be bothering us anymore.

Wet Mess   Maybe

Sue   hopefully

Wet Mess   probably

Sue   definitely

Wet Mess   certainly.

The green room door opens, **Midgitte** *walks in and joins them sitting.*

Midgitte   Sorry I'm late, was a really long night last night.

Rhys   Tea?

Midgitte   Oh I shouldn't kiss and tell.

Lilly   I hate to rush you, but sometimes we really must.

Midgitte   Well fine, I hate to rush, but sometimes we really got to do it, if you're wondering what it's like to fuck a bridesmaid, a bride *and* her dog who carried the rings, on a tiny little cushion, in the pantry of the wedding venue you're booked to sing in… All you have to do is ask.

Wet Mess   Well how was it.

Midgitte (*gives response.*)

Rhys   Now that is tea.

Midgitte   I'll just have water, thanks, and sorry I'm late.

Rhys *gets up to get some water for* **Midgitte***.*
Rhys *drops the glass of water and it smashes.*
They all turn and look at them.
Midgitte *helps clear it up.*

Rhys   Sorry, it's just today.

Midgitte   I know, today really is the day.

Rhys   Look, are we sure this is the right thing to do? What if it is a bit much?

Sue   You can't be getting cold feet now, surely.

Rhys   Our plans, they just feel…extreme.

Lilly   Extreme, what they are doing to us is extreme.

Sadie   Being worried about the gas bill, that's extreme.

Wet Mess   Being groped in the club, that's extreme.

Lilly   Not being hired cus you have a vagina, that's extreme.

Midgitte   Hey hey hey, lets not discredit Rhys' emotions please.

Rhys   Thanks Midgitte.

Midgitte   Rhys, look, you're being a pussy. And not the good, tough, survives-through-it-all type of pussy, more the old-school, stays-at-home-and-doesn't-fucking-take-risks type of pussy. But, that is well within your right, agency and all that.

Rhys   Well, I'm not the only one worried, I've already heard the whispers that this is going to fuck up their –

Ms Sharon *and* **Chiyo** *walk in, briefcases in hand, barging through to the kitchen, no room to sit so they sit on the counter. They have all the energy of people running late.*

Ms Sharon   Oh oh sorry we are late, blah blah blah the busses these days blah blah –

Chiyo   Oh the Central Line blah blah blah

Ms Sharon   the congestion

Chiyo   my digestion

Rhys   tea –

Ms Sharon   no more tea, let's just get down to business.

Chiyo *sets up a presentation stand and puts flipboards onto it.*
Chiyo *takes a little lecture pointer out.*

Ms Sharon   Now, as has been previously noted, today is the day.

Ms Sharon *nods at* **Chiyo***, who turns to a board that says 'TODAY IS THE DAY'.*

Ms Sharon   We have called in sick, taken the day off, told the bar we ain't coming in, and are here to complete the mission.

Chiyo   But Ms Sharon, could you remind us of that mission.

Ms Sharon   Thank you Chiyo, I absolutely will.

Chiyo *turns to a board that says 'THE MISSION'.*

Ms Sharon   We have had enough. We are tired of pay disparity, the comparisons, the pressure, the stupid little teenagers bloody *yaas-queen*ing and the *hunty-sashay*ing, and there comes a time where we must do the risky things in order to help the greater good. Some may call us villains, but I, I like to think of ourselves as change-makers, and isn't that truly one and the same thing. And today the change we are making is clear…

Chiyo   The mission.

Chiyo *turns to a board that says 'TO KILL HIM'.*

Ms Sharon *pauses. Looks at the board. Back to the cast. To the audience. To the board. Back to the audience.*

Ms Sharon   To kill him.

The cast do a nervous gulp. They drink their drink in unison. A weird, choreographed moment, like it was over-rehearsed. **Wet Mess** *is happy they nailed it.*

Sue   We are really gunna do this.

Ms Sharon   Oh my Sue Gives A Fuck we really, truly are. As it has been aforementioned previously stated, prior discussed, the art form we once loved is changing, and not in that natural way, but in the way that is driving everyone fucking nuts. Like *Big Brother* leaving Channel Four, or Worcester sauce crisps being nowhere to be fucking found. This change ain't good. No one likes this change. Why the hell would you fucking take the best packet of crisps straight off the shelf? No warning? No care?

Chiyo (*coughs*)   Ms Sharon, the brief.

Ms Sharon   Right, yes. Queer bars are closing as mega tours run by straights are thriving. Hen dos multiplying as weird experimental art spaces are shutting. Drag as an expansive, rule-defying, gender-bending, punk protest – is well, becoming sanitized, sanctioned, and following a rule book that we didn't set.

Chiyo   And then what happens Shazza?

Ms Sharon   Drag as an advert, as a money-first, art-second career, as a killing, and I think we are gunna be left for fucking dead.

Ms Sharon   Drag selling banks.

Chiyo *turns to a board that shows a weird joke version of a drag queen with NatWest.*

Ms Sharon   Drag selling Uber Eats.

Chiyo *turns to a board that shows that.*

Ms Sharon   Drag selling fucking nuclear bloody weapons for all I know.

Chiyo *turns to a board that shows* **Ms Sharon** *riding a nuclear weapon.*

Chiyo   The effect?

Chiyo *turns to a board that says 'THE EFFECT' with a little pyramid on it. On the pyramid at the top is 'DRAG QUEENS ON THE TV' and they are drinking champagne and fighting each other, and then loads of other drag performers drowning below.*

Ms Sharon   Good old-fashioned trickle-down top-down fucking economics.

Chiyo   And no one likes a top when it's down.

Ms Sharon   A small one per cent fighting for an even smaller coin that's shrinking and shrinking as the standard of who gets that coin becomes smaller and thinner and whiter and art becomes a rat race and I fucking hate rats… So we gotta do something about it.

Chiyo   Hands up if you feel like the industry has changed and become harder to work in the last two years? Hands up if you feel drag is more mainstream?

Lilly   Yeah, I mean some drag.

Chiyo   Hands up if you've still experienced a hate crime on the way back from work?

Ms Sharon   This just won't fucking do!

Chiyo *turns to a board – it says 'THE PLAN!'*

Chiyo   The plan stays the same, we ambush the oil rig the target is currently residing on. We take him hostage. And then we kill.

Sadie   Just like that?

Chiyo   Just. Like. That.

Midgitte   We're really gunna do it.

Lilly   I should hope so.

Rhys   Today is really the day.

Sue   It really is.

Wet Mess   It's finally the day.

Sharon and Chiyo   Let's fucking 'aveeee it!!!!

The scene shifts. As everyone cheers, **Chiyo** *and* **Midgitte** *and* **Sharon** *exit.*

The cheers are overshadowed by the sound of helicopters above, a battle ground, an army taking place.

The cast respond, by adding an army cargo jacket, or removing their pants to show short short cargo pants. A punk glitter tank breaks through the kitchen wall with **Chiyo,** **Midgitte** *and* **Sharon** *at the helm. Fucking the gun of the tank/taking poppers/doing something like that.*

Cabinets are removed by the cast as camoflauge falls out of them.

Mock roly-polies with dips added in across the stage as kitchen chairs are turned into barracks to hide behind.

Walkie talkies and binoculars out.
Smoke bombs thrown.
It's a big action movie, and the European staccato kitchen is
disappearing for a camp, full-scale army mission.

Sadie   Let's go!

Sadie *runs out of the green room. She is the one cast member*
in full femme, Destiny's Child-inspired army camouflage outfit.
Completely impractical. Everyone else resembles elements of army
within their clothing, layered or edited from their previous look.
Sadie *is a glimpse of the high femme version. The drag version.*

The cast are spread out.
Midgitte, Sharon *and* **Chiyo** *on the tank.*
Lilly, Sue *and* **Sadie** *are on top of the green room, binoculars on,*
toy snipers looking out. Passing a joint along.
Rhys *and* **Wet Mess** *behind a makeshift barrack.*

Sadie (*over the noise of the scene*)   Today, really is the day!

Lilly (*shouting too*)   It really is today!

Sue (*shouting*)   Today, it really is!

Chiyo   I DON'T KNOW WHAT I'VE BEEN TOLD

All   I DON'T KNOW WHAT I'VE BEEN TOLD

Chiyo   THE ART OF DRAG HAS BEEN BOUGHT AND SOLD

All   THE ART OF DRAG HAS BEEN BOUGHT AND SOLD

Chiyo   WHEN SOMETHING'S ROTTED GIVE IT THE BOOT

All   WHEN SOMETHING'S ROTTED GIVE IT THE BOOT

Chiyo   AND FUCKING DESTROY IT FROM THE ROOT

All   AND FUCKING DESTROY IT FROM THE ROOT

Chiyo   SOUND OFF

All   SASHAY AWAY

Chiyo   SOUND OFF

All   TIME TO PAY

Gun shots, cast excitement, reveling in it all.

Ms Sharon   Oh nothing gets me going like a good killing, Midgitte.

Midgitte   That's good to know Shazza.

Ms Sharon   It's the anticipation, the planning, the theatrics, oh the theatrics, makes me feel like I'm a Bond girl.

Midgitte   The franchise depends on you.

Ms Sharon *just sings one powerful extended note/phrase of 'Goldfinger' over the noise.*

Rhys   You ever think we are going too far?

Wet Mess   Yeah, Sadie could have lost at least one of the earrings…

Rhys   No, like, killing, him you know, he's a legend.

Wet Mess   Legends die too, we are just speeding it up.

Rhys   I don't know, it just feels…like, reactive.

Wet Mess   This whole fucking thing's reactive!!

Sue   Has anyone got eyes on the target?

Sue *pointing out to the auditorium.*

Lilly   Yes yes, I see him! Right there!

All   Where?

Lilly   Right there, at about four o'clock.

Wet Mess   I can't see him.

Lilly   Wait, sorry, no, that isn't him – that's just a bouncer blocking a femme lesbian from a club!

Chiyo   Easy mistake to make Lilly!

Sadie   Wait, wait, I think I got eyes on him! Over there!

Sue   You sure?

Sadie   I think that's him, either that or it's a drag queen getting touched up by a straight man whilst performing, I can't tell.

Chiyo   There he is! There he is! Next to the oil rig!

Midgitte   Where?

Sue   Oh I see! Left of the oil rig, right of the gravestone, sat bang in the middle getting his hair and make-up done.

Rhys   What does the gravestone say?

Sue   Wait, let me zoom in, uh, it says, 'HERE LIES THE DEATH OF AN ART FORM, ANOTHER VICTIM TO CAPITILISM, MAY IT REST IN PEACE'.

Midgitte   Ahhhh, let's get him!

The cast in unison pull out big dildos, hairspray bottles, hair straighteners, whatever things can be associated with queer/drag culture and look menacing but aren't actual violent weapons. They begin to act in unison, and prepare what looks like a jump onto the target.

All   Three, two, one –
LET'S KILL THE TARGET!

The cast jump, roll, fall, run into new spots in unison.
Smoke bombs erupt.
In formation, they do an army-like dance, march, choreographed work that shows them travelling and becoming militant and unison in finding and capturing RuPaul.

The dance is heating up, the crew are becoming more and more unified and intense and attacking.

The puppet version of RuPaul is lowered in as the cast come closer and closer with their weapons.

Closer and closer.
Closer and building.
Building and closer.

They freeze in action.

In this freeze-in-action, the cast will pause the show, and explain that in order to continue they will need tips from the audience.

This will include getting card machines out and negotiating how to get tips from richer members of the audience.

This is real money used and then split up as actual tips for all freelance workers on the show that week.

They then resume the action.

Rhys   This is it, today is the day.

Sadie   Today, really is the day.

Rhys   I didn't think it would need to come to this, but god does it feel good to get this close.

Sadie   To finally take back

Rhys   to have agency,

Sadie   to have power,

Rhys   to get down to…

They go to chop up RuPaul but the lights strobe.
Out of RuPaul's head is money.

Rhys   …business.

RuPaul's head-money spurts out –
Rhys *leads a strip-like costume and scene change centred around the money –*
As the act changes.

On the dismantling of the kitchen
After a long and difficult few days spent wrangling over how to smoothly transition out of a full working kitchen, into a boardroom, and then a queer utopian dreamspace, it occurred to us that within a performance that talks honestly about labour it was not only important to show the physical work required to dismantle an entire kitchen but that there is actually pleasure and meaning for an audience in watching the labour-intensive act of transformation carried out by the cast and crew. So the transition became about the material and temporal reality of taking apart one space in order to make way for another.

Act One: Beginning of the kitchen dismantle and view to the green room

Act Two: Dismantling of the kitchen by the cast and crew

Act Two: The Business

(A writer's note: this act is mainly made up of real-life interviews with the cast. This was heavily inspired by Scottee's Putting Words in your Mouth *and also Paula Varjack's* Show Me the Money. *These are questions about how they feel as workers in drag, the effects of RuPaul on the industry, competition and capitalism. I have chosen to not immortalise these interviews here, as they should be specific to the context of the show and location. Yet if you were to put on this play, you would interview the specific group of nightlife performers you have for this part.)*

As the money starts to fall from RuPaul's head, bursting out, money falls from above too; in fact money spurts everywhere.

The stage starts to be dismantled by the cast.
The cast are workers, this is them working.

Some may be doing the heavy lifting, **Midgitte** *may be just sitting there, watching everyone else work, looking every now and then like they want to, then not, but they are changing the set/tidying up the mess that has occurred.*

Someone sweeps money into a bin bag, janitor style.
Within that change, someone dumps bin bags downstage.

Wet Mess *appears from the bin bag, choking and spitting out money, a fully-formed businessman, the kind who stinks of aftershave and has too much slicked hair. An eighties stockbroker who has all the stocks in evil shit.*

They crawl out, poisoned by the money, and take centre stage.

Wet Mess *lip syncs pre-recorded interviews of the cast discussion about the labour of their jobs.*

Eventually, one by one, the cast join too. Lip syncing their parts.

Ms Sharon *is tired of the business talk.*
She doesn't want to listen.
She takes off her jacket to hint at something underneath, something more.
She sings a slowed-down, gorgeous hint of 'Sound of the Underground'.
Epic, overpowering the lip sync, all we can hear,
As the cast leave,
Sharon *is alone, singing,*
'It's the sound of the, sound of the underground.'
The palace of Act Three is lowered in as she belts.
It arrives.
She looks.
She looks back.

Ms Sharon   Well, you better come back after your fucking fag break.

She exits.

End of Act Two.

Interval.

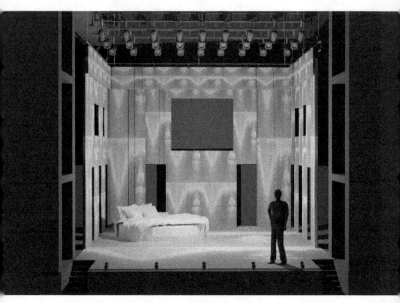

Act Three: The Fabric Palace and bed

Act Three: The Fabric Palace with lights

On the Fabric Palace

Following the hard, straight edges of the kitchen, the fabric palace is a space that's soft and forgiving to hold the performers and the acts they perform in the second half of the show. Once the last pieces of the kitchen have been pushed off stage, the palace floats down from above and defines a shift to a new kind of performance, and an imagined queer future. We were very inspired by Pink Narcissus and its heavenly dreamlike vibes.

Act Three: The Dream / Their Arrival

(Writer's note for Act Three: this is part-devised by the cast. We identified one cast member who could play as the host/compere, and co-wrote the text with them; here this is **Sue***. However, the rest of the cast were given two-to-three minutes to create a piece of their own. This should show who they are as a performer, yet using theatre to bring something new. Act Three becomes this specific cast's cabaret night, and we watch it unfold.)*

The palace of Act Three is draping the stage.
Act Three feels like a dream. Their vision. Their awakening. If Act One was what theatre wants, and Act Two was everything gross in the world, Act Three is about showing the holy from the rubble. The rest from the chaos. The performers in their fullest, in control, no fighting, no struggle, them in ease and power. Imagine a Greek gathering of kinds, one where they luxuriate in their art.
Soft drapes, mixed with the fag ash of a club.
A neon sign in the middle of a pile of pillows.
Perfume from a toilet attendant.
Cigarettes turn to cigars.
Silk robes to hide the costumes.
Aristocrats but ones that have fucked loads of people openly and proudly.

This is why the club must stay alive, so we do not lose the magic.

The audience walk in after the interval.
The performers are in luxurious robes covering their outfits.
They are always present in the space, unless needing to change.
They are all here right now.
Sue *is on the bed, cast gathered around her.*
Wet Mess*, dressed as an old-style painting, feeding* **Sue** *a grape.*
Sharon *and* **Chiyo** *up high rolling a cig.*
Midgitte *the cherub runs around the stage laughing, spraying perfume, in on the joke.*

Harmonious singing, angelic vibes, **Sue** *decides to speak.*

Sue   Welcome darlings, welcome back. A lot's changed, a good chunk of the audience have left, I'm in a gown. Can we have a moment for the attire?! It's not easy being beautiful, you know. Well I suppose you don't know that's why I'm in the gown. Hell of a fabric to clean. Although I can't bring myself to clean off the stains anyway, I mean that's someone's kids. Give me a whoop if you're a Kensington local?! Yeah so cleaning is like…something's dirty but you don't throw it away…like what you do to money.

Let's get to know one another. Give me a whoop if you're an LGBTQIA+ person! Give me a whoop if you're a heterosexual person! I am of course joking, heterosexuals you're more than welcome here. You're welcome everywhere, that's how privilege works.

I was quite excited to perform at the Royal Court, the Royal Court. I thought I've made it, mother you can return my calls I'm a star. And I am. But it turns out that a star here is paid 570 pounds a week for eight shows and a shared dressing room! And to be honest, all this structure, and explanation, and action of a play just really isn't my cup of vodka.

So I asked Siri for the answer in the break, I said, Siri, what is the answer? And Siri said: me, it's us.

Why would we come here, and not do what we do best…

The club.

Takes a long sip of something.

Oh that's cheap, you see, when the world above starts to panic, starts to wonder how to survive, they always turn to the ones that never stopped being on fire. The ones who have survived it all.

To make magic whilst on fire is a real skill.
To turn water into wine is a gift.
To be in the world of the underground – or lucky enough to know it, even to glimpse it. Well that's why you bought a ticket.

The cast do some fanning around **Sue**, *kinda joking kinda serious, going 'la, la la, la , la, la, la', moving the bed that holds* **Sue** *into her final hosting spot, laying around her and she speaks.*

Sue   I was there, when the first gay club started to show its ugly face. Poison the pure grounds like a fissure to the bum. It's like it was just a second ago. Eighteenth century – give or take an hour – of course there was probably some gay shit going on before that, as long as there's sunlight there's nightlife, and when there's nightlife someone's gonna be fingering someone.

But properly recorded, orally – or other less enjoyable methods – was the eighteenth century.

Molly houses they called them. Because that's what they called us. Places to fuck, to sing, to marry, to fuck, to dance, to socialise, to fuck. Put us in the bad parts of town, bad knows bad, but the one I knew, the one I was fisted in for the very first time, by this remarkable French guy actually, used butter as lube back then, not as effective but same outcome, well that was in Mother Clap's Molly House in Holborn. Ran by Margaret Club.

Sundays were notorious, couldn't tell which way was up and whose crumbling ball sack was whose. A good night out can do that.

Rumour even has it, Margaret used to run the club for pleasure and not profit…
Ha! Imagine that.
What a confusing time…

Anyway darlings, history-making and queers is like poppers and butt play – sure you can have one without the other, but damn it makes so much sense when it's together. And speaking of history,

our first performance is from someone truly making it. Changed
the scene forever, and for the better. Make some noise for Sadie
Sinner the Song Bird!

By the time **Sue** *has finished,* **Sadie** *is ready to re-enter from the
top of the stage. Dramatic entrance, makes way for the egality of*
Sadie Sinner.

Sadie *performers her act, which is a love letter to herself, about
what the Cocoa Butter Club gave her.* **Sadie** *is dressed in a pastel
blue classic burlesque outfit, she swings on a heart-shaped swing
as a piano jazz riff blends with her Mum singing a Zambian
lullaby. This then shifts in to different clips of previous audio
descriptions at the Cocoa Butter Club describing* **Sadie** *and her
outfits. Lauryn kicks in and* **Sadie** *begins a striptease. As the
striptease progresses, a recorded voiceover of* **Sadie** *reading a love
letter to her younger self plays. The movement material is built
around dancing the parts of your body you love the least. The act
finishes with a final reveal and* **Sadie** *announcing the Cocoa Butter
Club as a final act of love to her younger self.*

Sadie *is carried away by* **Chiyo** *and* **Rhys***, leaving* **Lilly** *centre
stage.*

Lilly *performs her act. In a departure from her usual comedy
burlesque, where she sends up stereotypes of East Asian women,*
Lilly'*s act is a classical burlesque striptease to Laosian music. She
is dressed as a Lotus flower and her moves are inspired by this.
The track then drops into an epic cinematic orchestration and* **Lilly**
does a striptease and then dances with burlesque fans.

Sue   Give it up for Lilly SnatchDragon!

That club, Mother Claps, well it got raided. Cops came in and
searched and stripped us, and not in the sexy way. Forty people
arrested and three of the men were hung, and, dare I say it, not
in the sexy way. The police didn't apologise but they do wear a
rainbow flag in the Pride march so I guess that's progress. They

just want to be involved don't they. Can't admit to wanting a little finger up the butt so do all this. FOMO but with weapons.

Banning things doesn't stop us though, the death penalty for buggery was abolished in 1861, but I'd been doing it for a hundred years by then, just ask Margaret Club. I met that remarkable guy again, you know the French one, I saw him in 1847 in an underground soirée. Soirée is the French word for chemsex party. Well he said he'd been doing it all underground since he last saw me, even more underground than before, cus they were arresting us. Just before I was being passed around to the next guy, he took his little toe out my ear and he could whisper in it, and you know what he whispered, he said:

'They can try and get rid of us, but we will always find a way to gather, and when we do, we will be even filthier than before.'

Speaking of filthy, do you want to see some Mess? Do you want to see something Wet?

Give it up for Wet Mess!

Wet Mess's act. *A baroque painting begins to shuffle downstage to some classical music. We realise that the face of the painting has been replaced with* **Wet Mess**'s *face and this painting is actually alive. At the end of the music* **Wet Mess** *throws the painting off, which gets pulled off stage, and goes into a dynamic and highly physical lipsync to a track called 'Flamboyant', playing with gender presentation with their physicality throughout. Towards the end a transphobic football chant comes in over the track ('is that a man or is that a woman') and* **Wet Mess** *enacts some football hooligan violence as both the perpetrator and the victim. At the end we hear a crowd cheering as though a goal has been scored and a confetti drop happens.*

This blends into **Rhys**, *who performs 'The Club is a Beast'. Dressed as a kind of futuristic Angel-meets-alien,* **Rhys** *enters to* *some fairly dark and gothic club music with strobe effect; the tone is horror and sinister. He then raps about the club as a place of church-like worship and holy sacredness as well as being a place of darkness, demons and a form of hell. There is a possible dance break involving the rest of the company and the end is yet to be made.*

Sue   Rhys's Pieces everybody! It's all just a lovely cabaret isn't it darlings? Are you all enjoying the show? I enjoyed a show once. One time. I think it was the Caravan Club, in 1934. They accepted us a bit more then, so I worried less about cops and more about the heat, you see it was so busy back then. Bustling. I started to see the divides in the gays, right. Cus it isn't just the gays, there's all of us, but divides start to form. Even back then, none of it is new. Posh aristocrats in some bars, people of colour hanging out in others, the squats where the real punks were going. All had their pros. Aristrocrats are okay if you have a ball gag. The aesthetes, the clones, the butches, the femmes, the lipstick lesbians, the leather daddies, the t-girls, the queens, the dolls, right down to the headless torsos and the Clapham gays, there's a place for each of us. Even when the world isn't dividing us we are doing it, but back then, from what I remember – botox has a nasty effect on the memory – we had choice. Which toilet to shit in. Opening up on every corner, every basement, ha, in the seventies you just needed to blink and there was a club for us to play in. Oohhh I don't wanna be to vulgar, it's not in my nature –

They mime giving fellatio.

– but I had lots of fun, lots of it, I missed that French guy though, a certain asscheek leaves an imprint on the heart, but sure I still had fun, and speaking of someone fun, someone that is too much fun –

Take it away Ms Sharon le Grand!!

Sharon *comes in dressed in a fabulous frock, does a Shirley Bassey/Phantom of the Opera-style cover of 'Cheeky Song (Touch*

My Bum)' by The Cheeky Girls. It's high glamour and surprisingly emotional.

Sue   It's weird being around as long as I have, you see it all changing, cycles and cycles and cycles, same thing just comes back around with a new face and a squeeze to let you know it never left. Kinda like that French Guy, you never forget a sweet embrace. You see I went to this bar, north of the river, to meet him. Yes, yes, he finally got back in touch. Only three hundred years since we first kissed, he texted me the other day, said 'Finally found your number, come meet me at this bar'. Well I went to the bar, I'm not going to let my pride get in the way of someone as gorgeous as him, and well the bar – it didn't exist. And neither did Frenchie. I looked everywhere for him but I couldn't find him. In fact, I couldn't find anyone there like me. Instead, I was greeted by a very confused estate agent who ran the property development. Now that estate agent was also a very good kisser, but that's besides the point. It made me think. A lot of the clubs I once loved are really nice flats now. Lovely carpets, a focus wall, enough air freshener so you can't quite smell the lingering odour that a bunch of queers leave behind. Culture wheel is always spinning, darling. And guess what, nightlife is out, and expensive housing is in, baby. Develop develop develop – and no need for these new accountants to have live entertainment, because Netflix is free on the smart TV. How does nightlife compete with television, with assimilation, with the promise of fame? But we don't go, we never go, we are always still here, we just find new ways to do it, to still be here, like cockroaches. Speaking of roaches, do you want another act? Midgitte!

*****Midgitte**'s act. **Midgitte** is dressed as a Cupid and possibly begins with some text that they have written. They then sing 'Hot Piss' and depending on technical allowances are raised up very high on a cherry picker. At the finale of the song a spray of (fake) piss shoots over the stage, hopefully creating a rainbow effect.*

*Into **Chiyo**'s act. **Chiyo**, dressed in a Prince-inspired hot pink New Romantic costume, enters to some Mahler and then*

strips to a grimy club track. Halfway through the strip the
track abruptly cuts. **Chiyo** *continues stripping in silence – it is*
deliberately uncomfortable. He then goes into a speech about
work, exploitation and oppression as a Brown trans man written
by Travis, which is both rallying and frustrated. It finishes with
him removing the final tear-away on his costume which proudly
exposes his genitals.

Chiyo   It's all work isn't it
Doesn't mean I don't enjoy it
But it's all work isn't it
Or doesn't mean I don't enjoy some of it
But it's still work isn't it.

Knowing that I can make you care about me,
By just using my body
That's work
Each line of definition
Sculpted in my stomach
Proving to you that I'm someone you deserve to keep

It's all work isn't it

This body was work
It takes work
I had to grind hard, be grinded down, grind on you
To get it.
No free shit for me
Fundraise by performing
Performing to get the money
To do the work to the body
To mean that I'm safe

It's all work isn't it

And then the applause comes
And it feels alright

When the applause comes
Means I must be doing this right
Sex sells,
And you can't drawl if you're too busy thinking
So don't think, just carry on touching.

Because that's how it's supposed to work
You applause
I strip
You cheer
I strip
You question nothing
I strip
You scream my name
We finish

And then you go home.
And I go home too.

Chiyo *stops stripping now and moves to directly address the audience.*

But then on my way home, I get attacked.
And I turn to look at someone to help me.
Someone that looks like that face I saw in the crowd, and they don't do shit
But they go home and switch on the TV and watch some fucking reality show about our lives,
Or enjoy a rainbow flag on their fucking football laces
Or use our language
Or take our culture
Or click at us at the fucking brunch –

But where the fuck is everyone when we actually need you.
What the fuck are you doing to keep us actually here?

Chiyo *regains composure.*

It isn't that this place magically saves us.
You can drape us in it all
But it doesn't mean we are in heaven
And if you only take from us,
Without wondering how to help us keep the lights on,
Then we will eventually fall
In between the cracks
Where maybe the true holy work is done
And wait for the next cycle to come...

Sue *covers* **Chiyo** *back in his clothes.*
The cast rise from the bed, singing Sound of the Underground *as a group.*
It's angelic.
A calling back to the underground.
The set rises back up,
They close out the show,
The red curtain re-drawn.

End of show.

On the green room
It felt important to us to create a space that was for rest and pleasure and not to hide that somewhere backstage. The space is camp and inviting. We dressed it with the performers' real belongings and the things they need before and after being on stage.

The wallpaper of the green room

On the Act Three costumes

For the third act we collaborated with eight costume designer/ makers for the eight performers, each designer creating a look with and for the performer that is specific to their act. All of the makers work predominantly in the world of drag, performance art, and the queer club scene. Many of them already had a close collaborative relationship with the performer they designed for.

Chiyo Act Three costume designed and created by Fancy Boy

Lilly SnatchDragon Act Three costume designed and created by Joey A Frenette aka Bourgeoisie

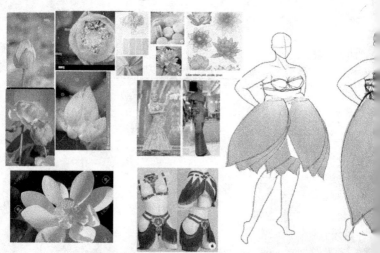

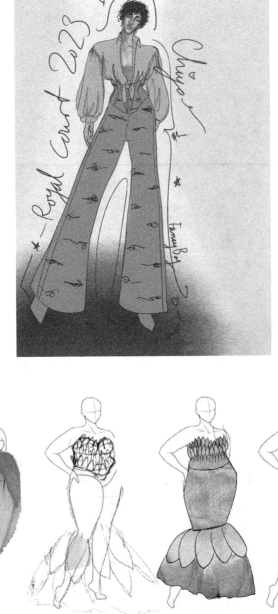

Midgitte Bardot Act Three costume designed and created by Alexandre Simões

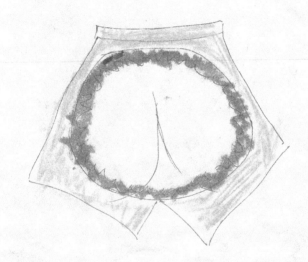

Midgitte Bardot Act Three pants designed and created by Alexandre Simões

s Sharon Le Grand Act Three costume designed and created by Max Allen ys's Pieces Act Three costume designed and created by Jivomir Domoustchiev

*Sadie Sinner Act Three costume designed and created by Bambi Blue
@ Trashy Planets*

*Sue Gives a Fuck Act Three costume designed by Sue Gives a Fuck
and created by Julian Smith; hat by Noel Stewart*

Purple velvet
Printed lobster carcus
onto shoe cover

hair horn piece.

make
outl
purple

Platform
under shoe
cover

Wet Mess Act Three costume designed and created by Lambdog1066

Afterword
By Lilly SnatchDragon

2022 marked ten years since I first started performing as Lilly SnatchDragon. I spent the majority of those years in London, and during that time, sixty per cent of the LGBTQ+ spaces in the city closed down. To my knowledge, at least eight of the queer venues I've performed in over the years are now closed.

Every single venue made an impact on me, a stop along the way as I built my identity as a queer person and as a performer. In some, I found a community for the night, in others I found family, and a home away from home for months and even years.

I don't know if there is any other job that is so interwoven with community and identity. Even though these were places of work, each one was also the nucleus of a family (not always a harmonious one, but what family ever is?). As much as my friendships and chosen families exist outside of those places, they are all bound together by them – by the work we did there, the memories we built, but also the shared grief of their loss.

The first venue to feel like home to me was Madame Jojo's, an iconic Soho drag and cabaret club that closed in 2014. I was still fairly new to the scene so I mostly stage-managed and it's where I really developed Lilly. At that time, Soho was known for being the queer centre of London and Madame Jojo's was completely representative of that vibrant culture. We'd do a show at Jojo's and head to Balans or Shadow Lounge for drinks afterwards. The streets would be full of queer people walking around in full drag and performers lived in flats above the bars. I didn't fully appreciate how significant Madame Jojo's was at the time, but looking back, its closing was like a death knell for Soho as a centre of queer community. As the queer venues closed, the less safe it felt. Friends began being attacked or verbally abused more frequently and Soho became the gentrified tourist trap that it is today. When the venues close, the community goes with them.

Alongside Madame Jojo's, I found the Black Cap in Camden, which closed in 2015. I started working there at the Meth Labs as part of the Family Fierce and eventually full-time behind the bar. I'd work the bar upstairs during the day and do shows downstairs at night. This was before Ru girls were everywhere, and the Black Cap was the only place you could see them in London. A small number of independent venues around the UK worked together to bring them over from the US, and unlike today, the profits and exposure that came with them were poured back into those queer spaces. I learnt so much queer history at the Black Cap. Working the bar, I met older people who had been coming there when homosexuality was illegal, when the windows were blacked out and everything was secret. I learnt about love and survival and met so many people that became lifelong friends. It was not glamorous – the dressing room was a corridor between the urinals and a dirty alleyway – but being there felt like a constant celebration of the freedom to be yourself and every night was like a family get-together. It was there that I got ready before going to accept my very first award (Best Newcomer at the London Cabaret Awards) and felt like a whole community was celebrating with me. To this day, if you talk to people who called the Black Cap home, they'll speak about it as if it was a family member that passed away.

Her Upstairs in Camden was the most recent venue I called home. It closed in 2019. In some ways it was a recreation of the Black Cap, with more of the diversity that was lacking there. At that point, *Drag Race* was really taking over and whatever benefits came with it were rapidly moving away from the community I was part of. In the shadow of that, Her Upstairs felt like a place for everyone it was leaving behind. I started LADs there with Lolo Brow and Scarlett O'Hora, celebrating AFAB and women performers, and I was in the very first The Cocoa Butter Club. It was the first time I performed and felt like my acts were actually understood. So many of the scene's biggest names, including many who went onto *Drag Race UK*, started at Her Upstairs. It wasn't trying to tick diversity boxes, it just wanted to give space to people who couldn't get it anywhere else. It was one of the rare places where you could go on your own and know that you'd feel safe and included. In 2016 my dad passed away, and the first New Year's Eve after that I was alone, and didn't know what to do, so I went to Her Upstairs. I went there again on my dad's birthday, got steaming drunk and sobbed on the dance floor, held by friends and strangers. Despite the very sad memories I have of the way that it closed, I remember it as a place that helped me heal. It's where I met my fiancé and one of the last events I attended there was the wedding of two of my best friends.

Looking back at my career, I realise how lucky I was, more than most in fact, to stumble across so many of these places and be part of so many communities. Yes, they were places of work, but they were also inextricably woven into every other aspect of my life and identity. Lilly is a product of those venues and the people that populated them, and it feels like I'm constantly searching for a way to be part of something like that again. Every time I host a show, I'm trying to recreate those spaces for the performers and the audience, because it feels like fewer and fewer people are able to experience them. A lot of the negative aspects of the scene that we explore in *Sound of the Underground* – exploitation by promoters, commercialisation and monetisation of drag, tokenism, etc – in my view come from the fact that these spaces are disappearing. If we don't have the physical spaces to come together and feel empowered, it keeps us vulnerable to these forces. It keeps us from finding our family.